JULIA B. LINDSEY

READING
ABOVE THE
FRAY

Reliable, Research-Based Routines
for Developing Decoding Skills

To all my students.
I wish I knew then what I know now.
May you always be readers.

Editorial director: Sarah Longhi
Development editor: Raymond Coutu
Senior editor: Shelley Griffin
Production editor: Danny Miller
Creative director: Tannaz Fassihi
Interior designer: Maria Lilja

Photos ©: 13: Courtesy of the author; 15: LWA/Getty Images; 32: SDI Productions/Getty Images; 33: Courtesy of Meghan Shea; 36: The Noun Project; 47, 64, 93, 146: FatCamera/Getty Images; 89: GlobalStock/Getty Images; 104: GoodLifeStudio/Getty Images; 115 top left: Courtesy of Meghan Shea. All other photos Shutterstock.com.

Additional credits ©: 24: Graphic by H. S. Scarborough from "Connecting Early Language and Literacy to Later Reading (Dis)Abilities: Evidence, Theory, and Practice," originally published in *Handbook of Early Literacy Research*, Volume 1. Reprinted by permission of Guilford Press; 26: Graphic by Nell K. Duke and Kelly B. Cartwright from "The Science of Reading Progresses: Communicating Advances Beyond the Simple View of Reading," originally published in *Reading Research Quarterly*, Volume 56. Reprinted by permission of John Wiley & Sons, Inc.; 101: *Excerpt from Daily Word Ladders, Grades 1–2*, text copyright © 2008 by Timothy V. Rasinski, illustrations copyright © 2008 by Scholastic Inc. Reprinted by permission of Scholastic Inc.; 134: Excerpt from *The Adventures of Captain Underpants*, text and illustrations copyright © 1997 by Dav Pilkey. Reprinted by permission of Scholastic Inc.
All rights reserved.

ISBN 978-1-338-82872-6

1 2 3 4 5 6 7 8 9 10   40   31 30 29 28 27 26 25 24 23 22

Scholastic Inc., 557 Broadway, New York, NY 10012

amazon.com

SXtSc7SnFD

Your order of May 31, 2022 (Order ID 113-4846064-1769857)

Qty.	Item	Item Price	Tot
2	Reading Above the Fray: Reliable, Research-Based Routines for Developing Decoding Skills Lindsey, Julia B. --- Paperback **133882872X** 133882872X 9781338828726	$29.99	$59.

Subtotal		$59.
Order Total		$59.
Paid via credit/debit		$59.

This shipment completes your order.

Return or replace your item
Visit Amazon.com/returns

0/XtSc7SnFD/ 2 of 2 //MCO9 CART B/second/3/0605-18:00/0605-06:30

Desk

JM2

CONTENTS

ACKNOWLEDGMENTS

This book stands on the legacy, knowledge, and friendship of so many incredible individuals, listed here and beyond.

To my students, from preschool to graduate school, thank you for allowing me to learn and grow with you.

To my mentor, Dr. Nell K. Duke, there are no words. It has been an honor to work with you. My only hope is to live up to your incredible example.

To my friends and reviewers, Dr. Laura Tortorelli, Kate Franz, and Elaine Shobert, thank you, thank you, thank you! I wouldn't have been able to write this book without your support.

To Brooke Childs and others at the Boston Public Schools, I'm honored that you trusted me to help your teachers and young readers. It has been a privilege to support your incredible work.

To Sharif El Mekki and others at the Center for Black Educator Development, I thank you for your support. There are no words to describe my deep gratitude, humility, and pride in working with you in the fight for equity and justice in education.

To the many other educators from whom I've learned, I stand in awe of all you do. My wish is that this book provides help to you and your colleagues. I thank you for inviting me into your classrooms.

To all my teachers and professors, again from preschool to graduate school, thank you for teaching me so much and preparing me to share all I've learned.

To Margery Mayer, Rose Else-Mitchell, Tara Welty, Ray Coutu, Sarah Longhi, and everyone else on the Scholastic team, thank you for working so hard on behalf of children and believing in my vision for reading instruction. I so appreciate you!

To my friends and family members, thank you for listening to my "reading rants" over the years, encouraging me, and always believing in me.

And to countless others who helped to shape this book, many, many thanks.

FOREWORD
by Nell K. Duke, University of Michigan

A few years ago, I had a conversation with an education leader that has stayed with me. The conversation touched on a number of controversial topics in reading education. For example, at one point in the conversation, I spoke against the dominance of the Simple View of Reading (Gough & Tunmer, 1986) in professional development. I argued for depictions of reading that capture a greater number and range of instructional targets, and that emphasize skills that bridge word recognition and language comprehension (views since articulated in Duke & Cartwright, 2021). At that point in the conversation, I believe the education leader associated my thinking with "balanced literacy," in part because many who embrace "the science of reading" heavily promote the Simple View.

At another point in the conversation, I expressed dismay at common approaches to teaching so-called "sight words," in which children are taught to memorize the words as wholes rather than fully analyze the graphophonemic (letter-sound) relationships in the words (e.g., Duke & Mesmer, 2018). At that point in the conversation, I believe she saw my position as aligned with the "science of reading" and in conflict with practices typical of "balanced literacy."

As the conversation wore on, the education leader seemed increasingly unsettled. Exasperated, she asked, "Which side are you on?!"

I am on the side of research. I consider it my professional responsibility to read, widely and deeply, studies on early literacy development and instruction. I use what I learn from those studies, as well as from my classroom experiences and the experiences of other educators, to make my best guess about any given question of practice. I am careful to check my guesses routinely with other experts, and I view my guesses as always subject to modification, elaboration, and/or nuance as additional research is published. This approach to questions of practice doesn't fit well with traditional notions of being on "a side" or in some literacy "camp."

In *Reading Above the Fray*, Julia Lindsey takes the side of research. Although many of the practices she recommends are aligned with what many currently associate with "the science of reading," such as explicit teaching of phonemic awareness and phonics, she doesn't recommend those for which there isn't a strong research base. For example, based on studies, she argues that phonemic awareness largely should be taught using letters, which is in contrast to some popular programs that teach phonemic awareness orally only while they purport to reflect "the science of reading." Similarly, Julia emphasizes the value of some practices that often aren't included in current conversations about "the science of reading" but have a strong research base, such as shared reading to develop concepts of print and extensive opportunities to read connected texts. Put simply, Julia doesn't align with a side, she aligns with research.

You'll see many signs that Julia's recommendations are grounded in research, including her discussions of specific findings, her citations of research, and her consistency of concluding recommendations with succinct reviews of research. You'll also notice that she recognizes the limitations of research—as when she uses phrases such as, "Though there is always more to investigate . . ." and "As I write this . . ." and "To my knowledge . . ." This tentativeness is typical of actual scientists but, unfortunately, not typical of many who claim to speak for "the science of reading."

There are a few other things I want to make sure you know about the author of this remarkable book:

- Although she is deeply informed by research, Julia's writing is highly accessible and her recommendations are eminently practical.
- Julia draws on the wisdom of practice as well as on research. You will notice that she refers to specific observations of and interactions with practitioners that have influenced her thinking, and it will be clear to you that she herself has been a classroom teacher.
- Unlike many voices in the reading education space, Julia isn't trying to sell you a program, and she isn't trying to make you feel like you need to sign up for her professional development services. On the contrary, she aims to provide enough information within the book to get you well on the way to more effective foundational skills instruction, as well as to empower you with references to other trustworthy books and free resources.

You have in your hands a great opportunity to grow in the way you teach foundational skills for reading. So, leave being on a "side" to next weekend's ball game, reserve "camps" for summer vacation, and get ready to align with research.

INTRODUCTION

Has scrolling social media these days made you want to cancel it? Have new state or district mandates made you think about finding a new career? Has the dramatic range of reading needs among your students made you wonder how you can possibly give all of them what they need? If so, you're not alone.

Barely a day goes by without journalists, podcasters, policy makers, and others coming up with new ideas about education. We can see from a mile away that some of those ideas are not going to impact us or our students positively. Others, though, do make us pause and reevaluate our practices. As exhausting and confusing as it can be to separate good ideas from not-so-good ones, it is something we need to do as professionals.

As exhausting and confusing as it can be to separate good ideas from not-so-good ones, it is something we need to do as professionals.

In recent years, many of those ideas have focused on early reading instruction. In response to staggering statistics about the percent of American fourth graders who are proficient readers (about 35 percent, according to the 2019 National Assessment of Educational Progress in Reading) and stories questioning current methods for teaching reading (e.g., those told in Emily Hanford's 2018 audio documentary, *Hard Words: Why Aren't Our Kids Being Taught to Read?*), there has been tremendous demand for changes in foundational reading instruction. Researchers, teachers, parent advocates, and state legislators have been justifiably fighting for more scientifically based reading instruction, especially in foundational skills, the basic skills needed to read words. But, like any fight, this one is messy. It's hard to know who is truly "right" at any given moment and what is important to embrace and what isn't.

A Little About This Book

In this book, I attempt to rise above the messiness—or above the fray—and help you focus on what the best of practice and the best of research tell us about instruction. Rather than fuel the fire, I'll get down to the question that's on all our minds: What do I need to know and do tomorrow and next week and next month to make sure my students can and want to read? Let's take a deep breath together and leave the noise behind. Above the fray, we'll create readers together.

This book is organized around three critical ideas:

1. Foundational skills are necessary for decoding, and decoding is necessary for fluency and comprehension.
2. Foundational skills must be taught with a clear purpose in mind.
3. To become proficient in word recognition, children need skills beyond those for decoding one-syllable words.

In Chapters 1 and 2, I make a case for the necessity of decoding. In Chapters 3 to 7, I get into the nitty-gritty of teaching individual foundational skills, the elements that are necessary for decoding: oral language, print concepts, phonemic awareness, alphabet knowledge, and sound-spelling knowledge (phonics). Think about these chapters as the essential elements that together allow for decoding and proficient word recognition. In each one, I discuss the foundational skill and its importance in reading. Then, I address instruction, offering clear, concise routines that explicitly match the purpose of instruction.

Chapters 8 to 10 are a little different. In Chapter 8, I focus on how the foundational skills described in Chapters 3 to 7 combine to allow children to decode words as effectively as possible. In Chapter 9, I extend beyond decoding by examining chunking—or the skills necessary for reading multisyllabic words: syllabication and morphology. Chunking is a specific type of decoding in which readers bring to bear their knowledge about larger parts of words and the sounds they represent. Lastly, in Chapter 10, I explore moving toward fluency and beyond.

A Note on the Instructional Routines in This Book

The routines in this book are all "swaps" that you can make tomorrow to trade out components of instruction that may not be serving you or your students. Think of these swaps as "more of this, less of that."

All the routines in this book take 15 minutes or less. That's because I firmly believe that foundational skills instruction should be quick and purposeful to be effective. Each routine is derived from research-based protocols to ensure they will help your students learn the targeted skill and support their long-term reading development. Although I provide routines for each skill, it is critical to always keep in mind the interconnectedness of foundational skills and the importance of supporting multiple skills at once.

While I firmly believe the routines will transform your instruction to be more efficient and effective, you still need a curriculum, a full scope and sequence, complete lesson plans, and assessments and ways to make sense of those assessments. And, of course, you need deep knowledge of your students. If you have a curriculum that you like and think is high quality, use the routines in this book to augment it. If you do not have a curriculum that you like or think is high quality, use this book to help you evaluate it, and share your thoughts with school leadership to start a conversation about finding a new curriculum. One place to start looking is on EdReports (at edreports. org/reports?s=ela).

Throughout the book, I also tell classroom stories and remind you to think carefully about motivation. And I always circle back to the four tenets of effective foundational skills instruction:

1. **Explicit and systematic** This means children are directly told what they need to know, and that we teach each component of a skill in a logical, orderly way.

2. **Efficient and effective** Foundational skills should never take all day. All the routines described are fast and research-based so we know there is a high likelihood of effectiveness. This does not mean that you should pick one skill and routine per day and assume children's needs are being met. Think about efficiency as realizing that you do not need to have an entire block of your day individually devoted to each skill if you purposefully teach each skill and integrate it in meaningful ways for reading and writing.

3. **Responsive to children's needs** Foundational skills instruction is best when targeted for a specific child, group, or class and their specific needs. This includes responding to assessment information and observations of children. It also includes bringing children's background, culture, family, and community knowledge into the classroom.

4. **Integrated with and applied to real reading and writing** No one wants children to be *phun phonics phact machines*, rather than real readers and writers. Remember, all foundational skills instruction is a necessary means to an end and must be applied to reading and writing that matters to children—reading and writing that is meaningful and purposeful. That starts by integrating all foundational skills instruction and then applying all skills to decoding.

A Little About Me

Admittedly, I am a foundational skills fanatic! A few summers ago, my friend and colleague Makael Burrell, director of the Freedom Schools Literacy Academy at the Center for Black Educator Development, summed it up best when, after watching me deliver a professional development session, he said to me, "I've never seen anyone who loves phonics as much as you. I didn't even know anyone loved phonics." Strange though it may be, I'd proudly sport a "Honk if you love phonics" bumper sticker on my blue Mazda sedan.

My journey to loving foundational skills began after I entered the classroom and realized the power of phonics. I watched, mesmerized, as most of my kindergartners learned to read words, then sentences, and then whole books. But, despite my best efforts at the time, I found myself unable to ensure all my students demonstrated the same learning: Some never quite seemed able to blend sounds to read words, some never quite moved beyond reading books with repeated patterns, some never quite applied all their isolated sound-spelling knowledge in actual books. These children's needs gnawed at me.

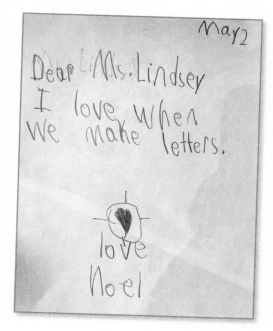

A note from one of my kindergarten students who loves phonics.

I left the classroom to study early literacy instruction at the University of Michigan, thinking I might focus on project-based learning and reading comprehension. Serendipity intervened, though, and I found myself and my advisor, Nell K. Duke, working with Brooke Childs, Director of Early Literacy of the Boston Public Schools. Brooke asked us if we could help her figure out how to bridge the gap between children's phonics experiences and their reading, rattling off many of the same challenges I'd noticed in my students' reading. This began a deep dive into how foundational skills were taught traditionally and how they may be taught better, based on research.

This book captures what I've learned so far, from reading too many journal articles to count, having the privilege of speaking with and listening to reading experts, developing and researching curricula and books, and observing and talking with incredible practitioners and the children I've taught.

This book captures what I've learned so far, from reading too many journal articles to count, having the privilege of speaking with and listening to reading experts, developing and researching curricula and books, and observing and talking with incredible practitioners and the children I've taught. I hope it helps make teaching foundational reading a little easier, a little more effective. And I hope that, just maybe, you'll learn to love phonics, too, if you don't already. Let's get started!

WHAT ARE FOUNDATIONAL SKILLS AND WHY ARE THEY IMPORTANT?

You might be surprised to learn, given how important foundational skills are, that there is not a definitive, universally accepted list of them. In fact, there is not even a definitive, universally accepted definition of them. (No wonder we keep having so-called "reading wars.")

Foundational Skills Defined

Several key publications have aimed to define foundational skills. For example, the *Report of the National Early Literacy Panel* (2008) defines them as skills that are highly or moderately predictive of success in reading. They include:

- Alphabet knowledge
- Phonological awareness
- Rapid automatic naming
- Phonological memory
- Concepts about print
- Print knowledge
- Oral language
- Visual processing

The Common Core State Standards for English Language Arts (2010) say foundational skills are what we should teach at each grade level to ensure children understand our written language. They include:

- Print concepts
- Phonological awareness
- Phonics and word recognition
- Fluency

And the *What Works Clearinghouse Practice Guide* (2016) says they are "skills that enable students to read words (alphabetics), relate those words to their oral language, and read connected text with sufficient accuracy and fluency to understand what they read." They include:

- Oral language and academic vocabulary
- Phonological awareness
- Phonics
- Decoding
- Fluency

All these definitions focus on skills foundational to word recognition because these are the skills that are most critical for reading success in the early grades. You'll notice several skills come up over and over: print concepts, phonological awareness, phonics, word recognition/decoding, and fluency. You might also notice some popular terms that are missing, such as phonemic awareness and high-frequency words. Does that mean those terms are unimportant? Certainly not! They instead tend to be embedded within skills.

One component of foundations missing from the three publications' lists is *morphology*. Morphology is the study of morphemes, the smallest units of meaning in language. Many words young children encounter have only one morpheme. For example, *ship* is a morpheme because we cannot split the word into smaller, meaningful parts. Most words older children (and adults) encounter, however, are multimorphemic. For example, *preview* is multimorphemic because it can be split into two smaller, meaningful parts (*pre* and *view*). So, knowledge of morphology is critical for multisyllabic word reading in English (Goodwin & Ahn, 2013; Nagy & Anderson, 1984; Zhang & Ke, 2020). We often call this skill *morphological awareness*, understanding how words can be broken into morphemes. Morphology might not show up in some lists of foundational skills because most teachers do not begin working with multisyllabic words until the end of first grade (or later). Nonetheless, it is foundational to proficient word reading of all types of words in English. (For more information, see Chapter 9.)

CHAPTER 1 • WHAT ARE FOUNDATIONAL SKILLS AND WHY ARE THEY IMPORTANT?

17

FOUNDATIONAL SKILLS AND TERMS RELATED TO THEM

Term	Definition	Examples and Extensions
Alphabet Knowledge	Connecting letter names, sounds, and forms	"The letter *B* spells /b/, like at the beginning of *ball*."
Fluency	Reading with accuracy, automaticity, and prosody	Reading like an adult with the appropriate speed and expression for the particular text
Morphology	Identifying and manipulating morphemes, the smallest units of meaning in language	"The word *helpful* can be broken into two parts, both for meaning and for decoding: *help* and *ful*."
Oral Language	Producing and comprehending spoken language, including vocabulary and grammar	Everything related to understanding and using spoken language
Sound-Spelling Knowledge	Knowing how to represent sounds in oral language with spellings	"The letters *o-u* can spell the sound /ow/ like in the word *loud*."
Phonics	Instruction in sound-spelling relationships	Practices that relate sounds to spellings to read and spell words
Graphemes	Written representation of a sound	Graphemes include individual letters and combinations of letters that spell phonemes.
Phonological Awareness	Identifying and manipulating units of sound in oral language	Manipulating words, word parts, and phonemes
Phonemic Awareness	A subset of phonological awareness—identifying and manipulating phonemes, the smallest unit of sound in oral language	"The word *dog* has three phonemes: /d/ /o/ /g/."

FOUNDATIONAL SKILLS AND TERMS RELATED TO THEM		
Term	**Definition**	**Examples and Extensions**
Phonological Memory	Holding information in short-term memory	Remembering the sounds in spoken language
Print Concepts	Understanding how to navigate print and that it holds meaning	"We start reading at the top left of the page."
Rapid Automatic Naming	Ability to rapidly identify a series of objects	Quickly identifying a sequence of random letters
Visual Processing	Ability to perceive, analyze, synthesize, and think with visual patterns	Discriminating visual symbols (such as letters)
Vocabulary	Having knowledge of words and their meanings	"The word *trustworthy* describes someone who tells the truth and is honest."
Word Recognition	Identifying a word (automatic, effortless, accurate recognition is the goal)	The goal: seeing the word *hot* and knowing it is the word *hot* immediately.
Decoding	One critical way to recognize words, using knowledge about sound-spelling correspondences	"/sh/ /o/ /p/ shop."
High-Frequency Words	The most common words in written English	Words such as *a, the, in, to, by*, and *for*

CHAPTER 1 · WHAT ARE FOUNDATIONAL SKILLS AND WHY ARE THEY IMPORTANT?

19

How Foundational Skills Help Most Children to Succeed

The Report of the National Early Literacy Panel (2008) and *What Works Clearinghouse Practice Guide* (2016) both emphasize that foundational skills need to enable later success in reading. There are three ways we can be sure foundational skills are necessary for most children to succeed.

1 Research has repeatedly found that certain skills are able to predict later outcomes in reading.

Studies continually find that early phonemic awareness and letter-sound knowledge predict decoding skills, which can predict reading fluency and reading comprehension (Caravolas et al., 2019; Lepola et al., 2016; Hulme & Snowling, 2015; Torppa et al., 2016). In other words, if children have foundational skills at an early age, they are more likely to become proficient readers in terms of fluency and comprehension.

Early phonemic awareness and letter-sound knowledge predict decoding skills, which can predict reading fluency and reading comprehension.

We also know that the reverse is true: Children who are not proficient readers in later years are likely to have had gaps in their foundational skills when they were younger. In a study of fourth graders scoring in the "below basic" category on the last National Assessment of Education Progress, researchers found these children demonstrated less automaticity, accuracy, and expression in word reading, both in isolation and in books, than their more proficient peers (White et al., 2021). As mentioned earlier, approximately 34 percent of fourth graders scored in the "below basic" category in 2019.

Another study, involving over 1,000 children, found that third graders who had solid foundational skills were about seven times more likely to pass the state's English Language Arts tests than their peers with weak foundational skills (Paige et al., 2019). Though we certainly know that standardized tests do not tell us everything about readers, we cannot ignore that these two studies suggest many, many children are not receiving the instruction in foundational skills they need to become strong word readers.

2 Research has also found that children's reading abilities improve when they receive instruction in foundational skills.

We know this from studies of grade-level classroom instruction, as well as studies of reading interventions. For example, there is widespread recognition that systematic and explicit phonics instruction is an efficient and effective way to teach word reading, and that phonics knowledge is critical for children to learn to read (Henbest & Apel, 2017; National Reading Panel, 2000; Torgerson et al., 2018). We know that instruction in phonological awareness in preschool through early elementary school improves reading skills (Bus & van IJzendoorn, 1999). We also know that phonemic awareness interventions can positively impact children's early reading, both immediately and even a year later, compared to their peers who didn't receive phonemic awareness interventions (Suggate, 2016).

The Mega Benefits of Meta-Analysis

The Bus and van IJzendoorn study and Suggate study cited in this section were meta-analyses. A meta-analysis is a systematic review of research about a topic. In a meta-analysis, researchers typically look for all the studies that assessed impact, often by comparing groups that received something (like a phonemic awareness intervention) to groups that didn't receive the same thing. Then, the researcher(s) takes all studies that meet his or her criteria and analyzes all the results together, using statistics. This lets the researcher make broader conclusions about impact. We can learn a lot from meta-analyses because they tell us what researchers across many decades and many types of studies have learned about how to impact something (like reading outcomes.) For that reason, when possible, I refer to the findings of meta-analyses throughout this book.

3 Understanding our written language and word recognition theories can directly explain the utility of each foundational skill.

We have a written system for our oral language. Text on a page directly represents oral language. To translate text into oral language, a child first needs to know that print matters and how to navigate a text. In other words, children need print concepts. Once children notice text, they need to know what oral language each word represents. We have an alphabetic language where letters represent sounds; therefore, children need to know sounds (phonological awareness) and letters (alphabet knowledge) to figure out what word each written word represents.

CHAPTER 1 · WHAT ARE FOUNDATIONAL SKILLS AND WHY ARE THEY IMPORTANT?

21

What Is a Deep Orthography?

An orthography is the spelling system for a language—and English has a deep orthography, meaning the relationship between letters and sounds is not direct. Languages with shallow morphologies, such as Spanish and Finnish, have consistent spellings for words and have a one-to-one letter-sound correspondence. In Spanish, for example, most spellings represent one specific pronunciation. For example, in *lo siento*, the letter *o* always spells the sound /long o/. In English, that's not the case. For example, *heed*, *hede*, *heid*, and *head* are all legitimate estimated spellings of the word /h/ /long e/ /d/ because *ee*, *e-e*, *ei*, and *ea* are all ways to spell the long e sound. But there is only one correct way to spell /h/ /long e/ /d/: *heed*.

In English, we have a *deep orthography* with both morphological and phonological elements. Therefore, children need to know a lot of sound-spelling relationships (phonics and morphology) and how to use these to read (decode) and spell (encode). Reading is not a natural process and applying all the knowledge described above to a text is challenging cognitive work.

Foundational skills enable proficient reading. As you read this book, keep in mind this summary of what they are and how they benefit children.

Foundational skills help children:

- navigate written text (print concepts).
- hear the sounds in language (phonological awareness).
- map those sounds to spellings (phonics knowledge).
- apply print concepts, phonological awareness, and phonics and morphology knowledge to reading (decoding) and spelling (encoding) to automatically, accurately recognize words.

Foundational skills allow children to become accurate, automatic word readers.

Foundational Skills Aren't Reading

It's important to keep in mind that foundational skills are not an end in themselves, but rather a means to an end. Proficient readers do not need to rely on foundational skills to recognize most words (though, when they encounter an unknown word, such skills certainly help). Mastering foundational skills makes them almost obsolete. The goal of foundational skills instruction is to give children the most efficient and effective path to fluent word reading so that they (and you!) can spend time and energy on comprehension and knowledge-building work.

Models of Reading

There are several prominent models of reading that help us understand how the components of reading unite to result in comprehension. These models are not instruction models. They are theoretical models to try to explain how reading works. Though we can glean important instructional implications from these reading models—they, by themselves, do not tell us what to teach. The models separate reading into two major parts, in addition to other complexities: the foundations of word recognition and language comprehension. These two processes do not necessarily develop together, nor do they lend themselves to different types of instruction and assessment.

The Simple View

One model of reading, which was developed over 35 years ago and is still popular today, is the Simple View (Gough & Tunmer, 1986). This model postulates that reading comprehension is the result of successful decoding and successful language comprehension. The researchers split those two abilities because they require different skills sets and knowledge to carry out successfully and they require different types of instruction and practice. Generally, most of us today think about foundational skills as the skills underlying *decoding*, which, according to Gough and Tumner (1986), is word

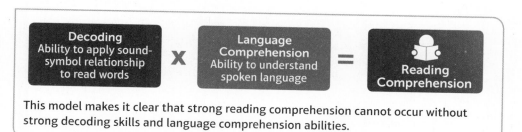

This model makes it clear that strong reading comprehension cannot occur without strong decoding skills and language comprehension abilities.

(Gough & Tumner, 1986)

CHAPTER 1 • WHAT ARE FOUNDATIONAL SKILLS AND WHY ARE THEY IMPORTANT?

23

recognition via letter-sound knowledge, both automatic word recognition and its precursor, sound-by-sound reading. This model reminds us that decoding is just as important as language comprehension in leading to proficient reading because you cannot possibly comprehend words that you can't recognize.

The Reading Rope

Dr. Hollis Scarborough (2001) built on the Simple View. She continued to delineate word recognition and language comprehension, but more precisely defined the subcomponents of them.

Scarborough separated decoding (using the alphabetic principle and sound-spelling correspondences to read words) from sight word recognition (automatic, accurate word reading). In her view, word recognition is key to skilled reading, and both the skills of word recognition and language comprehension work together.

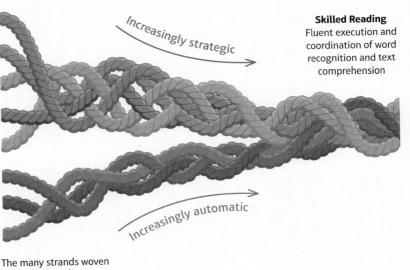

Language Comprehension

- **Background Knowledge**
  (facts, concepts, etc.)
- **Vocabulary**
  (breadth, precision, links, etc.)
- **Language Structure**
  (syntax, semantics, etc.)
- **Verbal Reasoning**
  (inference, metaphor, etc.)
- **Literacy Knowledge**
  (print concepts, genres, etc.)

Word Recognition

- **Phonological Awareness**
  (syllables, phonemes, etc.)
- **Decoding**
  (alphabetic principle, spelling-sound correspondences)
- **Sight Recognition**
  (of familiar words)

Increasingly strategic

Skilled Reading
Fluent execution and coordination of word recognition and text comprehension

Increasingly automatic

The many strands woven into skilled reading

(Scarborough, 2001)

The Active View

Reading research has continued to advance. Duke and Cartwright (2021) built on the Simple View, the Reading Rope, and more current research to offer the Active View of Reading (see chart on the next page). In this model, we see some familiar skills from the Simple View and the Reading Rope, such as:

- Phonological awareness
- Decoding skills
- Recognition of words at sight

However, instead of just thinking about how word recognition and language comprehension function, Duke and Cartwright build on research from many disciplines to incorporate other factors that determine children's success in reading, such as self-regulation and bridging processes between word recognition and language comprehension.

Duke and Cartwright extended the Simple View and the Reading Rope. But their model contains many of the same core elements related to word recognition.

Though the models continue to increase in complexity, just as research continues to advance, they all say approximately the same thing about word recognition—that it is a result of foundational skills/decoding and is a critical component of reading. These stable, decades-old ideas are also reflected in the definitions of foundational skills presented thus far.

Though the models continue to increase in complexity, just as research continues to advance, they all say approximately the same thing about word recognition—that it is a result of foundational skills/decoding and is a critical component of reading.

CHAPTER 1 · WHAT ARE FOUNDATIONAL SKILLS AND WHY ARE THEY IMPORTANT?

25

The Active View of Reading

This is a reader model. Reading is also impacted by text, task, and sociocultural context.

WORD RECOGNITION

Phonological awareness
(syllables, phonemes, etc.)

Alphabetic principle

Phonics knowledge

Decoding skills

Recognition of words at sight

ACTIVE SELF-REGULATION

Motivation and engagement

Executive function skills

Strategy use
(word recognition strategies, comprehension strategies, vocabulary strategies, etc.)

BRIDGING PROCESSES

Print concepts

Reading fluency

Vocabulary knowledge

Morphological awareness

Graphophonological-semantic cognitive flexibility
(letter-sound-meaning flexibility)

READING

LANGUAGE COMPREHENSION

Cultural and other content knowledge

Reading-specific background knowledge (genre, text features, etc.)

Verbal reasoning
(inference, metaphor, etc.)

Language structure
(syntax, semantics, etc.)

Theory of mind

(Duke & Cartwright, 2021)

Though language comprehension is not the focus of this book, I want to highlight a critical component recognized by the Active View: cultural and other knowledge (information and knowledge learned through experiences, such as daily activities within one's cultural groups [e.g., Duke & Cartwright, 2021]). It is vital to recognize the importance of children's cultural and other knowledge they bring to the classroom as assets for further learning. Though there is limited research (so far) about how a child's cultural knowledge interacts with instruction and development of foundational skills, we should strive to teach foundational skills in a way that uplifts and affirms all children's experiences, languages, and knowledge.

WHAT THE MODELS HIGHLIGHT			
Literacy Terms	The Simple View (1986)	The Reading Rope (2001)	The Active View (2021)
Phonological Awareness		✓	✓
Decoding/Phonics	✓	✓	✓
Fluency		✓	✓
Vocabulary	✓	✓	✓
Comprehension	✓	✓	✓
Knowledge Building		✓	✓
Language Structures		✓	✓
Verbal Reasoning		✓	✓
Self-Regulation			✓
Motivation			✓
Executive Function			✓

(Based on Chanter, 2021)

CHAPTER 1 · WHAT ARE FOUNDATIONAL SKILLS AND WHY ARE THEY IMPORTANT?

27

Taken together, what do these models convey about the skills foundational to reading? They:

- tell us that the components of reading are skills related to word recognition and skills related to comprehension.
- distinguish between word recognition and language comprehension, but the latest model most clearly identifies skills that contribute to both processes.
- "boil down" reading to word recognition and language comprehension, but the latest model reminds us that reading is more complex than just the product of two distinct processes.

Using all three models for inspiration, as well as the most up-to-date research, let's zoom in on the most important foundational skills and what instructional practices should lead to word-reading success.

Why Word Reading?

Reading words proficiently is the backbone of reading proficiency, and learning to do it in the primary grades is essential. Ideally, skills build from year to year, with children achieving more fluency and more comprehension as they move up the grades. Instruction in foundational reading skills in the early grades is particularly important, ensuring children develop fluency without the need for later intervention. One reason this is particularly important is that research tends to find that, in reading, "the rich get richer." Children who experience success in reading build more and more skills as they read more and more texts, while those who do not experience early success tend to have more and more difficulties compared to their peers ("Matthew Effects," Cain & Oakhill, 2011; Stanovich, 2009). Children who are not proficient word readers in the early grades tend to be non-fluent readers in later grades (Hernandez, 2011; Landerl & Wimmer, 2008). Foundational skills help children to become proficient word readers by decoding words—or using their knowledge about spelling and its relationship to sounds to read unknown words. Each foundational skill is a critical element of decoding. I'll dive more into the criticality of decoding in Chapter 2.

Foundational skills help children to become proficient word readers by decoding words—or using their knowledge about spelling and its relationship to sounds to read unknown words. Each foundational skill is a critical element of decoding.

Two More Critical Principles: Joy and Cultural Responsiveness

In addition to the four tenets of effective foundational skills instruction above, I offer two more critical principles. Foundational skills instruction can and should also be joyful and culturally responsive.

Joy

Foundational skills instruction should be joyful. Joyful, however, doesn't mean that every day feels like a birthday party. It does mean, though, that children should be engaged in purposeful tasks that they can carry out confidently and successfully—for example, you might play favorite songs or read favorite books to learn more about particular letters or letter sounds. You might pair up friends to work together to build words containing particular sound-spelling patterns. Joy can also mean celebrating small victories along the way, like learning to decode a new word or reading a text with fluency.

To bring joy to your foundational skills instruction, focus on the purpose of that instruction: to help children become passionate, proficient readers.

Think about it: Foundational skills allow a child to take random markings on paper, signs, and screens and translate them into words. The foundations of reading are fascinating. Just look at what they allow us to do—and more to the point, what they allow children to do. I'm sure we all have stories about children who came into our classes knowing very little about written language, but who left as readers. That is powerful. That brings joy to those children and to us, as their teachers. Though teaching foundational skills may seem mundane at times, remember it is magic for a child. To bring joy to your foundational skills instruction, focus on the purpose of that instruction: to help children become passionate, proficient readers—and have some fun along the way. After all, it is so cool to learn to read words! Throughout the book, I'll point out some research and experiences that challenge our notions that skills-based instruction isn't engaging for children. Foundational skills can and should be joyful, engaging, and motivating.

CHAPTER 1 • WHAT ARE FOUNDATIONAL SKILLS AND WHY ARE THEY IMPORTANT?

29

Cultural Responsiveness

Foundational skills instruction can also be culturally responsive. I certainly can't offer all the answers to questions about culturally responsive instruction. But I can offer some hope. Some people say that culturally responsive instruction and foundational skills instruction are contradictory. This does not need to be the case, and to prove it, I want to tell you about an organization that is integrating both types of instruction brilliantly.

In 2019, I began working with the Center for Black Educator Development, led by Sharif El-Mekki, to develop a new model of Freedom Schools, a culturally responsive summer literacy program. The Freedom Schools Literacy Academy aims to support Black children in becoming proficient, prolific readers through culturally responsive, research-based literacy instruction.

In the summer of 2020, amid the COVID-19 pandemic, children who participated in the program met with teachers for about 20 hours on video chat, primarily doing explicit foundational skills instruction and reading in decodable text. These children grew in many ways, making gains in word reading, oral reading fluency, listening comprehension, and positive racial attitudes (Center for Black Educator Development, 2020; Lindsey, 2021). At the end of the program, children were more likely to be reading on grade level (according to national norms; University of Oregon, 2020) *and* more likely to say they liked and were proud of their racial identity. (Important note: All the children in the program identified as Black or Latino.)

There are many exciting things to say about the Freedom Schools Literacy Academy and the brilliant leaders and educators behind it. But, for our purposes, I want to stress that foundational skills instruction does not have to be separate from culturally responsive teaching—it should be a part of it, empowering children to become readers while uplifting their identities.

Culturally responsive instruction isn't a "nice to have" or an add-on, it's an essential part of all instruction, including early reading

What Is Culturally Responsive Instruction?

Culturally responsive instruction is teaching in a way that recognizes and honors children's backgrounds and experiences as assets for learning (Gay, 2010; Ladson-Billings, 1995). Teachers who practice it intentionally support and validate students' knowledge, language variations, and perspectives (Morrison et al., 2008). They deeply believe in children's abilities to succeed (Ladson-Billings, 1995), and transform school experiences to facilitate that success by leveraging children's knowledge and empower them to use it (Gay, 2010).

instruction. Research shows that children comprehend texts more deeply when those texts include characters and topics that match their cultural background knowledge (Bell & Clark, 1998). However, culturally responsive instruction is about much more than using representative texts. It aims to challenge students and help them succeed. It also aims to leverage and affirm their cultural knowledge to support cognitive development (Hammond, 2014). Authentic culturally responsive teaching is not easy, but I strongly encourage you to learn more about it for the benefit of your practice and your students.

A Note About Me and Cultural Responsiveness

I'll do my best to talk with you about culturally responsive foundational skills instruction, but know that I do not have all the answers. I've made a conscious choice to include this section despite that because cultural responsiveness is so critical to all that we do in classrooms. I invite you to learn more from others far more knowledgeable than me about cultural and linguistic responsiveness and anti-biased education. Here are recent professional books that address cultural responsiveness, which I highly recommend:

Cultivating Genius: An Equity Framework for Culturally and Historically Responsive Literacy by Gholdy Muhammad

Start Here, Start Now: A Guide to Antibias and Antiracist Work in Your School Community by Liz Kleinrock

Revolutionary Love: Creating a Culturally Inclusive Literacy Classroom by Kamania Wynter-Hoyte, Eliza Braden, Michele Myers, Sanjuana C. Rodriguez, and Natasha Thornton

Culturally Responsive Teaching and the Brain: Promoting Authentic Engagement and Rigor Among Culturally and Linguistically Diverse Students by Zaretta Hammond

CHAPTER 1 · WHAT ARE FOUNDATIONAL SKILLS AND WHY ARE THEY IMPORTANT?

31

CHAPTER 2

DECODING AND ITS ESSENTIAL ELEMENTS

There's magic in the moment that letters become something more. We've all seen it happen, we've all had the chance to marvel at the beauty of that moment for a child. Melissa Scafaria, a kindergarten teacher in Michigan, had the chance to see it more and more, thanks to a swap in her weekly routines. Skeptical, but curious about their power, Melissa introduced her kindergartners to a small number of meaningful, decodable texts matched to her phonics curriculum, in addition to the texts she typically used in her reading instruction. When using decodable texts, she also shifted her instruction and prompting to focus children on decoding words. The effect was almost immediate. "Kids could decode words!" she said. Not only that, but across texts and contexts, Melissa's students were also more confident and engaged when encountering new words in a way she'd never seen before. Kids decoding words, that's the magic—for them to realize they've been taught the information and skills they need to uncover a word all by themselves—and that they can do it whenever they read, for any purpose.

Decoding Defined

When readers decode a word, they use knowledge of the connections between graphemes (letters) and phonemes (sounds) in that word. The most common decoding strategy is sound-by-sound decoding. Chunking words into parts using syllables or morphemes is also a decoding strategy.

Sound-by-Sound Decoding

/b/ /a/ /l/

Chunking

/play/ /ing/

As laborious as it may sound to us as skilled adult readers, beginning readers must have the chance to decode many words over and over to move toward automatic word recognition. After several successful attempts at decoding a word, a reader will memorize the word's spelling, pronunciation, and meaning. The process of applying sound-spelling knowledge to analyze a word (i.e., decoding) is a critical step in creating an orthographic map (Chambrè et al., 2020), which allows a reader to commit words to long-term memory (Ehri, 2020; Kilpatrick, 2015). Then, the reader can recognize that word automatically. Decoding is the bridge between phonics knowledge and proficient word reading.

Melissa's experience doesn't need to be unique. By shifting her practice from focusing on phonics and reading separately to focusing on children's decoding, she opened the door for her kindergartners to build the skills of strong early readers—without sacrificing joy, engagement, or comprehension work.

What's the Difference Between Phonics and Decoding?

Phonics is a type of instruction, specifically instruction in sound-spelling relationships and in using those relationships to read and spell. *Decoding* is how to use sound-spelling relationships to read. Phonics instruction should include decoding. However, decoding sometimes gets overlooked in phonics instruction because so much time is spent on sound-spelling relationships. I'm making a big deal out of decoding on its own to focus us on helping children know *how* to use sound-spelling knowledge.

A critical stop along the way to reaching our big goals for readers is *teaching children to decode using a sound-by-sound strategy*. This is most effective for single-syllable words. Decoding may seem like the "flavor of the month" in reading circles right now, but it isn't a trend. Decoding is a "big deal" precisely because it should be.

The Science of Recognizing a Word and Orthographic Mapping

For a long time, there has been debate about how readers recognize words. Do they recognize the whole word? Do they use portions of it? Do they use all its letters? Though there is always more to investigate, current research using eye-tracking technology and brain imaging provides a consensus that, to recognize a word, even proficient readers use its letters, and the position of those letters in relation to all the other letters (Grainger, 2008; 2018).

We, as proficient readers, recognize words by reading letters, even though we might not realize it. So, it is essential that we teach children how to recognize words that way, too.

Further, though context can help proficient readers recognize a word, they do not need it to recognize most words (Stanovich, 1980). No matter where you see them—in a book, on a billboard, in a chalk-written message on a sidewalk—you can automatically recognize simple words such as *cat* and more complex words such as *catastrophe*. And that is the goal. Automatic, accurate, effortless word recognition. In other words, we, as proficient readers, recognize words by reading letters, even though we might not realize it. So, it is essential that we teach children how to recognize words that way, too.

Proficient word recognition—in which a reader can automatically, accurately, effortlessly recognize thousands of words—is a must-have for fluent reading. And fluency supports comprehension, taking readers from the small moment of recognizing a word to the goal of reading instruction: comprehension. Oral reading fluency and decoding accuracy also relate to comprehension of a text (Juel et al., 1986). Longitudinal studies continually find that letter-sound knowledge predicts decoding skills, which predicts reading fluency and comprehension (Caravolas et al., 2019; Lepola et al., 2016; Hulme & Snowling., 2015; Torppa et al., 2016). Although successful comprehension of a text requires more than just accurate word reading, research and theory indicate that accurate oral word reading supports successful comprehension (Amendum et al., 2018).

Word reading can be efficiently and effectively taught in part through explicit instruction in systematic phonics (de Graaff et al., 2009; Henbest & Apel, 2017; Torgerson et al., 2018). Ideally, that instruction leads to proficient,

What About Irregular Words?

Even irregular words can be orthographically mapped. The word *you* is unusual; however, you can teach children that, in this word, all three letters spell a long-*u* sound. At present, there is no reason to believe that our brains process irregular words differently than other words, so we should learn them the same: by connecting letters to sounds. To recognize irregular words, you can remind children about their irregular sound-spelling connections. See Chapter 7 for more on irregular words.

fluent readers who can read mostly by automatic, accurate recognition of words' pronunciations and meanings from memory (Ehri, 2005).

So how do children likely learn to recognize words automatically and become fluent readers who can comprehend complex texts? Current theories suggest that, to read an individual word, a child needs to create an orthographic map by linking the word's orthographic information (spelling) to its phonology (pronunciation) and semantic information (meaning) (Ehri, 2005, 2014, 2020). When a reader creates an orthographic map of a word, she retrieves the word's meaning and pronunciation automatically, effortlessly from memory, when she encounters the word. To create orthographic maps and their sight word vocabulary, readers need to form connections between spellings and pronunciations, and that is achieved through decoding (Ehri, 2014; Share, 2004).

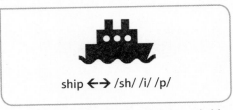

ship ←→ /sh/ /i/ /p/

Orthographic map of the word *ship*

Decoding Is the Best In-the-Moment Option

When proficient readers encounter a new word, they can, and do, use lots of different information to try to read it. Decoding is not the only way to recognize an unknown word. Readers rely on letters, knowledge of morphology, knowledge of other words, the sentence's syntax, and context to "solve" a word. Researchers from the 1960s and 1970s noticed that readers use multiple sources of information when reading words, which led to a theory that children became good readers by predicting words based on the text's meaning, the sentence's syntax, and some visual information (Clay, 1968; Goodman, 1970). These ideas took off and became the basic underpinning of many current instructional practices in reading. There are three basic issues with using those ideas to drive our instruction.

1. Skilled word readers do not need to use multiple sources of information to solve words (Ehri, 2014; Foorman et al., 2016). Though readers can use multiple sources of information, proficient readers are primarily paying attention to each letter and the words' orthography to read. By contrast, poor readers seem to rely more on context than orthography (Pratt, 2020).

2. The most efficient and effective way for readers to recognize new words is through decoding (Miles & Ehri, 2019). We need to build efficient, effective foundational skills instruction so that our students have more time and cognitive energy for other aspects of reading. We want to use the most effective and efficient instruction possible.

3. Children naturally want to look at pictures and also predict words using context. A major goal of decoding instruction is to instead focus children on using letters to decode words. That doesn't mean that children won't, or shouldn't, continue to use context to understand texts. It means that we can help children use a more effective strategy (decoding) to recognize the words in the first place.

Decoding Is the Best Long-Term Option

In addition to helping children solve a word in-the-moment, decoding is best for long-term word recognition. It supports the creation of orthographic maps (see page 35), allowing children to store a word's spelling, pronunciation, and meaning in memory (Ehri, 2014; Kilpatrick, 2015). When we give them the opportunity to decode a word several times (usually from one to eight times, depending on the word, context, and child's knowledge), they can store the orthographic map they create in memory (Bowey & Muller, 2005; Nation et al., 2007; Share, 2004). Critically, knowledge of and repeated exposure to spelling patterns in words seems to facilitate orthographic learning. Orthographic learning is much faster than simply memorizing every word in the English language (Cunningham et al., 2002; Hiebert & Fisher, 2016; Share, 2004).

You might be thinking, "But if the goal is automatic word recognition, isn't that basically the same as memorization?" Though it is possible to memorize words, research estimates that young readers learn several thousand words a year, and it is simply impossible to memorize that many words. Furthermore, memorizing words in the short term and/or using other information to predict words does not help children create orthographic maps (Rastle et al., 2021). So even if children can identify a word, they don't necessarily store it in long-term memory.

Decoding Is Motivating

Decoding might not seem that spectacular (though I hope after reading this chapter you think it is). Especially when done in isolation, it might seem like "skill and drill," and it might seem incredibly hard for some children. But decoding a word correctly can be highly motivating and joyful. Just like the brief story at the beginning of this chapter, that "Yes! I read that!" moment is thrilling for a student (and a teacher) and far more likely when we've given children the right tools (such as decoding) and the right words (such as words they can read based on their knowledge of orthography).

The seemingly simple act of helping children learn to decode, and read lots of words they can decode, can bolster their skills and therefore, their motivation.

Reading performance and motivation to read influence each other. Good reading leads to reading motivation, just as reading motivation leads to good reading (Toste et al., 2020). To support that relationship from the start and to meet our goal of successful and motivated readers, we need to recognize that the seemingly simple act of helping children learn to decode, and read lots of words they can decode, can bolster their skills and therefore, their motivation.

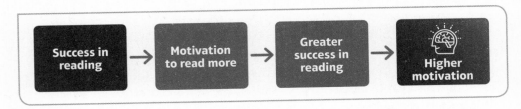

The Elements of Decoding

Acknowledging how word recognition works and why it is so important, we need to make choices that support it. That means teaching children how to decode familiar words. What does it mean to teach decoding? It means teaching first (or simultaneously) the elements of decoding.

Decoding is the product of phonemic awareness and knowledge of sound-spelling correspondences, which encompass these skills and subskills:

1. **Oral language and vocabulary:** Children need to know lots of words and their meanings to make sense of written language.

2. **Print concepts:** Children need to know what print is to use it to read.

3. **Phonemic awareness:** Children need to be able to blend and segment phonemes to attach them to spellings.

4. **Alphabet knowledge:** Children need to know the alphabet to work with our written system.

5. **Sound-spelling knowledge:** Children need to know how letters and letter combinations represent sounds to read words.

A panda can grab plants to chomp.

To read the word *chomp*, a child needs to know:

- The symbols on the page represent words
- *ch* represents /ch/, not /c/ and /h/
- *o* represents /o/
- *m* represents /m/
- *p* represents /p/

Sounds can be said one at a time and then slid through/blended to say a whole word.

These skills, applied together, allow a child to decode an individual one-syllable word. Without them, he or she will not be able to recognize and make sense of the word. They are slightly different from the wide range of foundational skills I discussed in Chapter 1. They are the skills that are most critical for word recognition by decoding.

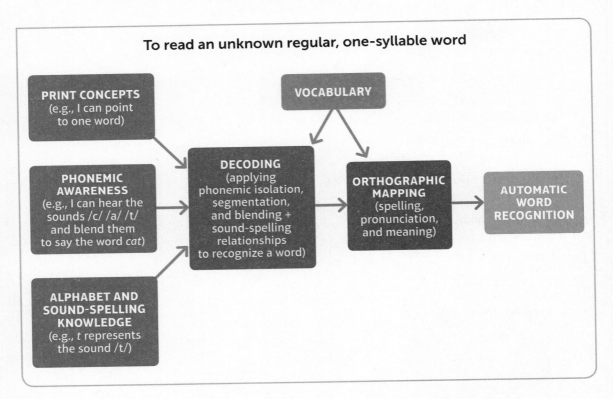

Bringing It Together

In Chapters 3 to 7, I go into detail about each of these elements, how they relate to decoding and reading, and what instructional swaps you can make to ensure you are teaching them as efficiently and effectively as possible. By making those swaps, you will ensure children become proficient one-syllable word readers, one major step in becoming fluent readers.

Element One:
ORAL LANGUAGE AND VOCABULARY

Building children's oral language and vocabulary skills is critical to their reading development. Those skills lay the foundation for them to understand individual words and connected texts. Though we often think about oral language and vocabulary as exclusively a part of comprehension work, they undergird all reading experiences, and we must consider how to support them throughout foundational skills instruction.

What Are Oral Language and Vocabulary, and Why Are They Important?

Oral language refers to all kinds of speaking and listening. It is the system we use to express knowledge, ideas, and feelings. In the broadest sense, oral language is the umbrella under which other knowledge falls, such as knowledge about phonology, syntax, semantics, morphology, and pragmatics. Here, I will explore syntax, semantics, and pragmatics for word reading. In later chapters, I will explore phonology and morphology.

When we talk about oral language instruction in the early grades, we often start by talking about vocabulary exposure and instruction. Vocabulary knowledge (semantics) is about knowing the right words to engage successfully in conversation or understand a text.

Domain	Focus
Phonology	the sounds in a language
Syntax	word order, grammar, and rules of a language
Semantics	the meanings of words, phrases, and sentences (sometimes called *vocabulary knowledge*)
Morphology	the smallest meaningful parts of words (morphemes)
Pragmatics	the social rules of language

Unlike many skills associated with reading, oral language develops naturally. Human brains are designed to enable us to talk. Researchers estimate that children recognize about 10,000 words by age five (Shipley & McAfee, 2019).

Despite that, researchers also know that it is helpful to support children's oral language in instruction. Instruction in components of oral language, such as vocabulary and syntax, can support reading comprehension (Silverman et al., 2020).

Early oral language skills also predict reading comprehension across much of development. Here are a few findings from research:

1. Preschool oral language (including vocabulary and listening comprehension) predicts third-grade reading comprehension (Lepola et al., 2016).

2. Kindergarten vocabulary knowledge predicts second-grade reading comprehension (Roth et al., 2002).

3. Second-grade listening comprehension (including vocabulary and grammar) predicts seventh-grade reading comprehension (Lervag et al., 2018).

Early oral language skills predict a child's ability to comprehend texts for many years to come. That makes a lot of sense considering that most oral language skills are about using and understanding different aspects of language, which can be applied to written texts.

But do oral language skills matter for word reading? This is a tougher question to answer. Recent research suggests that, for children learning to read in English, oral language knowledge (i.e., vocabulary, syntactic, and morphological knowledge) in kindergarten may not predict later decoding or reading comprehension (Caravolas et al., 2019). Other research, however, indicates that vocabulary knowledge is likely crucial to word recognition (e.g., Beck et al., 2013; Foorman et al., 2016), especially for multilingual learners (August et al., 2020). Like all foundational skills, we can think of oral language skills and vocabulary as one part of what children need, but not everything. By intentionally supporting children's exposure to complex language, you are likely to support their word reading and comprehension.

Less Foundational Skills Overload, More Language- and Reading-Rich Instruction

Though most of this book will focus on code-related skills, such as decoding, phonemic awareness, and morphology, it is not a call for an all-day phonics curriculum. Creating phonics robots who can't understand texts is obviously never the goal! Code-focused foundational skills are just one part of supporting children in the functional goals of instruction: actual reading and writing of complex text. Just as it is important to focus on teaching word recognition, it is important to focus on ensuring your classroom remains a language- and reading-rich environment.

When you start focusing on word reading, it's all too easy to overdo it. You might be tempted to create a time of day for each foundational skill: a phonological awareness block, a phonics block, a fluency block, and so on. This won't serve your students for a few reasons:

1. Those skills must be applied in concert. They aren't discrete, individual skills that proficient readers apply individually, so they shouldn't be taught that way.

2. Research does *not* support hours and hours of foundational skills instruction. For example, the *Report of the National Reading Panel* (2000), which is often cited to justify tons of isolated phonemic awareness instruction, says that "more is not necessarily better" (NRP, 2000). Instead, the researchers found the most impactful phonemic awareness trainings were less than 20 hours total across a school year or intervention.

3. Reading is not just about word recognition. Students need many other types of instruction to be successful readers.

On the next page is an example of how you might structure time for foundational skills throughout the day.

A POSSIBLE DAILY ROUTINE FOR TEACHING FOUNDATIONAL SKILLS		
Time Frame	**Instructional Moves**	**Possible Instructional Point in the Day**
30 minutes	Whole-class integrated foundational skills instruction, small-group and/or individual instruction as needed	Phonics Time
10–25 minutes (depending on need and grade level)	Small-group or individual instruction in which students apply the skills in activities, such as reading decodable texts, engaging in shared readings and interactive writings, and engaging in other specific needs-based instruction	Literacy Centers or Stations
20 minutes	Support independent or partner activities to build foundational skills, such as reading decodable texts, doing word and picture sorts, and playing digital foundational skills games.	Literacy Centers or Stations
40–60 minutes	During writing instruction, focus on all aspects of writing, and include some targeted opportunities for supported application of foundational skills, such as attempting spelling of unfamiliar words.	Writing Time
20–40 minutes	While engaging in deep comprehension work in complex texts, include some targeted opportunities for supported application of foundational skills, such as practicing reading along with an adult fluent reader.	Read-Aloud
Throughout the day	Support application of foundational skills in reading and writing tasks outside the literacy block, such as using decoding skills to read word problems in math or making connections to science in connected decodable texts.	

Bringing It Together

Oral language and vocabulary develop over our entire lifetimes. As such, no matter what grade level you teach, you can focus on improving children's oral language and vocabulary. To learn more about supporting children's oral language and vocabulary development, and to learn principles of great instruction (including lots of vocabulary and knowledge development), check out the following resources.

- *Bringing Words to Life: Robust Vocabulary Instruction, Second Edition*, by Isabel L. Beck, Margaret G. McKeown, and Linda Kucan
- What Works Clearinghouse Practice Guide: *Teaching Academic Content and Literacy to English Learners in Elementary and Middle School*
- What Works Clearinghouse Practice Guide: *Improving Reading Comprehension in Kindergarten Through 3rd Grade*
- *Melissa & Lori Love Literacy Podcast* by Melissa Loftus and Lori Sappington. Try episode 42, 66, or 78 to start.

This is not an exhaustive list, but just a place to get started.

Element Two:
PRINT CONCEPTS

Understanding basic print concepts is the underpinning of being able to read written text in any language. Take this text:

我喜欢阅读

If you are like me, unable to read Chinese, you can't decipher this text for many reasons. Before even trying to identify the individual characters, you'd need to know a few critical things about reading Chinese, such as:

- Characters, not letters, comprise written Chinese.
- Chinese characters generally represent a syllable of a spoken word. They can also represent a physical object, abstract idea, or pronunciation of a word.
- The direction of written Chinese is not always the same.
- Written Chinese often contains little punctuation.

In other words, I do not have a good chance at making meaning from these characters because I do not know where to begin to read, where to go once I've begun, what the characters represent, or where the sentences begin and end. This is how pre-readers feel about all written language! Knowledge about how print operates and how it holds meaning allows children, at a very basic level, simple access to the wide world of written language. Despite the importance of print concepts, they tend to be overlooked, taught non-systematically, or assumed a part of children's knowledge after preschool. Just like learning to read, children do not naturally learn print concepts simply from exposure to print. They need instruction.

What Are Print Concepts and Why Are They Important?

Children have understandings about text when they arrive in our classrooms, and it is essential for us to build on those understandings through instruction. Before they can read, they need to know that words are meant to be read and understood. Print knowledge is knowledge about written language, both in how it operates and how it's spelled, or its orthography. Broadly, it refers to knowledge about print concepts (also called concepts of print) and alphabet knowledge. In this chapter, I explore print concepts. I'll dive into alphabet knowledge in Chapter 6.

Print concepts relate to how printed texts operate, starting from very basic concepts ("print holds meaning") and moving to sophisticated ones related to genre and text features. The goal of instruction in print concepts is for children to use the knowledge they gain to navigate and create texts. We often think about aspects of written language such as directionality (e.g., in English, we read from left to right) and conventions (e.g., in English, we capitalize the first letter of the first word in a sentence). These basic understandings about how our written language works are essential for children to access any text.

Early knowledge of print concepts is highly predictive of reading success, even when controlling for variation in other early predictors of reading, such as phonological awareness (Levy et al., 2006). Many children start to understand print by reading with caregivers and by seeing everyday print (e.g., menus and greeting cards) and environmental print (e.g., logos and signs). Children who haven't interacted much with books need high-quality instruction in print concepts, beginning on Day 1 in kindergarten. This instruction will ensure they have the print knowledge they need to become proficient readers (Justice & Ezell, 2002). High-quality explicit and systematic instruction can accelerate children's understanding of print concepts (Justice et al., 2010; Nevo & Vaknin-Nusbaum, 2018) and their reading success (Piasta et al., 2012).

Children's ability to notice, identify, follow, and explain basic concepts of print follows a somewhat predictable developmental trajectory that can be organized into four categories:

1. print meaning
2. text organization
3. sentence organization
4. letter and word knowledge

Like most foundational skills, individual print concepts are not that useful on their own. Your goal should be to help children develop enough understandings about print to be able to track words and lines of text. After all, a child cannot decode a word without first being able to identify a word within the text.

Examples of Environmental Print

CATEGORIES OF EARLY PRINT KNOWLEDGE	
Category	**Definition**
Print Meaning	• Understanding that print holds meaning • Noticing print (e.g., in the environment, in texts, in pictures) • Noticing and identifying purposes of print
Text Organization	• Identifying a book's front and back covers • Identifying title, author, and illustrator • Understanding directionality (e.g., left to right, top to bottom, page to page, return sweep)
Sentence Organization	Understanding concepts such as: • Punctuation • Letter and word spacing • Capitalization
Letter and Word Knowledge	• Having alphabet knowledge • Identifying (and contrasting) letters, words, and sentences • Tracking words in text along with speech (one-to-one correspondence of words)

The table on the next page shows the general progression of children's understandings of print (Justice & Ezell, 2002). Unlike some skills, print concepts do not necessarily develop in this specific stairstep; however, this table gives a general idea about how this development tends to progress. First, children need to know that print exists and is worth noticing. Young children do not tend to even look at text without us encouraging them to do so (e.g., Justice et al., 2005). Then, they learn the features of books and how to navigate the text they contain. Keep in mind, children do not need to master these skills before they begin instruction in the alphabet. Tracking print, for example, tends to depend on some awareness of letters and syllables, so it may not fully develop until children are also engaged in alphabet instruction (e.g., Mesmer & Lake, 2010).

A Developmental Progression of Concepts of Print for Pre-Readers and Early Readers	
EARLIEST	Noticing print (including environmental print)
	Understanding that print contains meaning
	Identifying basic book parts (front and back covers, spine, pointing to title)
	Identifying print on a page
	Pointing to a letter
	Understanding basic directionality (e.g., left to right, beginning at the top left, ending at the bottom right)
	Noticing contextualized print (print in pictures)
	Understanding the function or purpose of specific print elements (e.g., title, speech bubble)
	Understanding more advanced directionality (return sweep, line by line, page order)
	Pointing to specific letters (and recognizing whether they're upper- or lowercase)
	Identifying (and contrasting) letters, words, and sentences (noticing spacing between them)
	Noticing punctuation
LATER	Finger pointing and tracking print (one-to-one correspondence of words)

As young children develop as readers, they learn more about how print is organized. Through repeated encounters with texts and explicit instruction, they learn more about conventions (e.g., punctuation and capitalization) and about the contexts and purposes for texts. They also learn more about specific types of texts, features of various genres, and graphics in informational texts.

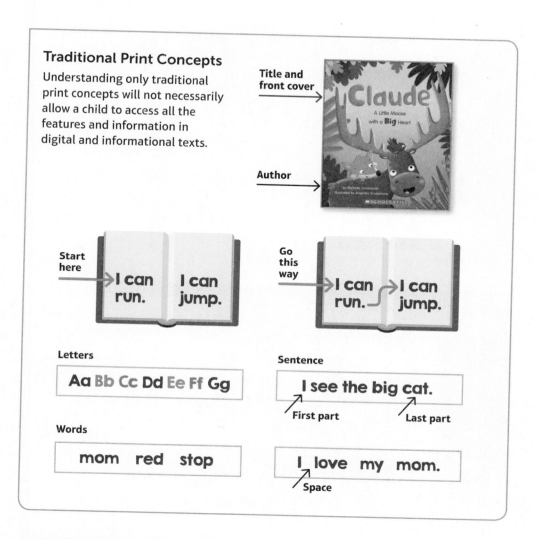

Traditional Print Concepts

Understanding only traditional print concepts will not necessarily allow a child to access all the features and information in digital and informational texts.

Title and front cover

Claude
A Little Moose with a **Big** Heart

Author

Start here

I can run. I can jump.

Go this way

I can run. I can jump.

Letters

Aa Bb Cc Dd Ee Ff Gg

Words

mom red stop

Sentence

I see the big cat.

First part **Last part**

I love my mom.

Space

A Wider View of Print Concepts

To read accurately and understand the myriad texts they will encounter, children need a wider view of print concepts that includes digital texts and graphics in informational texts. By explicitly and systematically teaching concepts like those, in addition to traditional print concepts, we can be sure we are supporting children in understanding how a wide variety of text types operate.

Digital Text

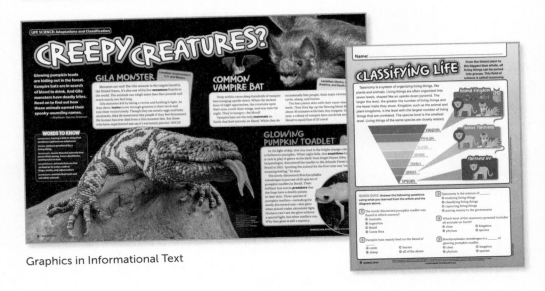
Graphics in Informational Text

Advanced work in print concepts likely continues throughout school and beyond. Though we do not typically think about knowledge of print concepts expanding across our lifetimes, it does. As proficient readers, it's not uncommon for us to encounter new types of text that we must learn to navigate (for example, reading a scientific journal article for work). In elementary school, we can support children in navigating and understanding some of the more advanced print concepts they will continuously encounter.

Concepts of Digital Text

Children are immersed in technology from a very early age. We might assume that means they are "digital natives" who do not need support in navigating or reading digital texts. However, don't assume all children today will know how to use digital texts. Though they might be able to play online games, swipe to new screens, and use photo filters before they join us in the classroom, they will not know how to navigate all forms of digital texts, nor know how to use all their features. To read even the simplest ebook, we need to understand how to navigate it—how to swipe, scroll, use arrows, etc. For more sophisticated ebooks and other digital texts, we need to know even more, such as how to activate and follow animations, listen to narration, write with a stylus, and so on.

As with print concepts, we need to teach children digital text concepts explicitly and systematically. This area is not well researched, but we can look to studies that exist on ebook reading for instructional ideas (e.g., Shamir & Korat, 2015).

What are digital text concepts? Beyond the ones listed above, we can't be quite sure because, again, the research is just not there yet. The next best thing is to think about digital text concepts alongside traditional print concepts. Below are some digital text concepts children need to navigate and understand ebooks (based on Javorsky, 2014).

DIGITAL TEXT CONCEPTS		
Category	**Concepts of Digital Texts**	**Traditional Print Concepts**
Navigation	• Holding a tablet, phone, or computer • Clicking to a new location, swiping to the next page • Following text across a page	• Book holding • Understanding directionality on and across pages
Icons	• Identifying icons • Using icons	• Noticing contextualized print • Identifying letters, words, and sentences
Animation	• Identifying and understanding picture or text animation as meaningful	• Understanding concepts of graphics
Narration	• Following narration or highlighting while reading	• One-to-one correspondence with oral and printed words

Concepts of Graphics in Informational Texts

The use of graphics is a major concept to consider including in your explicit, systematic foundational skills instruction in kindergarten, first grade, and second grade. Children tend to skip graphics in text (Norman, 2010), losing out on essential content. Understanding graphics helps them comprehend informational texts. See some concepts of graphics that tend to develop in early elementary in the chart at left (from Duke et al., 2013).

In addition to understanding concepts of graphics, children need to understand the basic types of graphics they will encounter and how they can extend their understanding of the text.

EARLY CONCEPTS OF GRAPHICS
Graphics can show action.
Graphics are created on purpose to help explain parts of or the whole text.
Graphics in a printed text do not change.
Graphics relate to the text.
Graphics can represent real things, but do not have all the same properties.

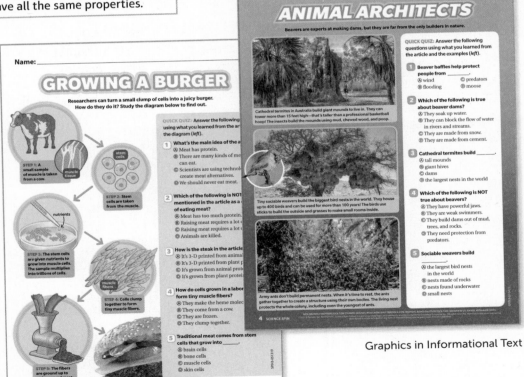

Graphics in Informational Text

Principles of Great Print Concepts Instruction

Taking what we know from research and practice, here are the four instructional principles for building knowledge of print concepts.

1 Explicitly and Systematically Address Print Concepts

Print concepts should be addressed in an explicit and systematic way to ensure that you don't miss any of them. Explicit, systematic instruction also gives each child the opportunity to learn exactly what each concept means. Use the developmental progression on page 52 as a starting point for a scope and sequence if you do not have one yet.

2 Follow an Efficient and Effective Routine

One of the most effective routines for building children's knowledge of print concepts is shared reading, which I will get into later in the chapter. This routine can take under 15 minutes a day and is supported by decades of research, so you can feel confident it will support your readers.

3 Respond to the Specific Needs of Children Based on Assessment

Like all instruction, instruction involving print concepts is best when it's driven by assessment results. It is likely that kindergartners will need instruction in many basic print concepts. Children in kindergarten through second grade will likely need an understanding of genre features and graphics. Children in all grades will likely need digital text concepts, depending on their experiences with technology.

To identify children's needs in basic print concepts, use an assessment such as Marie M. Clay's *Concepts About Print,* Second Edition (2017). You can extend that assessment by asking children additional questions about genre features, graphics, and digital texts. For example, if you are planning to use tablets for reading, you could say:

- Show me how to hold the tablet.
- Turn on the tablet and navigate to the bookshelf app.
- Show me how to go to the next page in our ebook.

Once you've identified your students' needs, address them using explicit, systematic instruction with the whole class, small groups, and individuals.

4 Support Print Concepts in Real Reading and Writing Contexts

Print concept knowledge is essential because it applies to real reading. In addition to shared reading, you can support children's print concepts in essentially any reading or writing experience. For children who need additional support, point out target concepts and allow children to practice them. If technology is available to you, consider asking your IT department for help in accessing a digital library that includes texts with features, such as audio with word and sentence highlighting, which will reinforce your explicit instruction.

Less Pointing to Text in Predictable Books, More Engaging in Shared Reading

Shared reading is a powerful technique with decades of research behind it, showing how it supports children's learning of foundational skills. It can improve oral language and vocabulary, awareness of print and knowledge of print concepts, phonological awareness, and word and letter knowledge (Eldredge et al., 1996; Lefebvre et al., 2011; Mol et al., 2009; Ukrainetz et al., 2000; Wesseling et al., 2017; Zucker et al., 2013).

One common way to support print concepts, especially one-to-one correspondence between spoken and written words, is teaching children to point to text in predictable, patterned, or repetitive books. We essentially ask children to memorize the words in those books and repeat them back as they point to each word and say it. At this time, there is little evidence to support that method of building word recognition, and some experts are concerned it might even harm or delay decoding (Bogan, 2012).

So, instead of using it, swap it for a technique that is proven to support the print concepts, as well as other foundational skills necessary for decoding: shared reading. Through shared reading experiences, you can bolster a wide range of children's foundational skills while explicitly, systematically supporting their knowledge of print concepts.

The Bus Ride

Each day we ride the bus to school.

We listen and follow every rule.

Inside we keep our hands and feet,

We always sit down in our seat.

We use quiet voices so the driver can hear!

This way we stay safe all year!

Example of text for shared reading.

An Effective and Efficient Routine for Shared Reading

Here is a routine for shared reading that you can use in one lesson or across multiple lessons. Research has found shared reading to be beneficial in whole-group and small-group settings as well as individually so you can use this routine in the way that works best for the needs in your class. Depending on how many questions you ask or concepts you focus on, this protocol can take from about 15 minutes for all three reads to about 15 minutes per read (45 minutes total, likely across days). Before you teach, you will also need to consider:

Text Selection

- If you are working on very early print concepts, pick a text that is print salient—containing printed words that draw children in with text that might be big, colorful, or bold.
- Check the text to ensure it has the feature you are focusing on. You can't teach children about punctuation, for example, if there isn't much punctuation for them to notice!
- Pick a text or portion of a text that isn't too complex. During the last portion of a shared reading, you will ask children to join you in reading, so aim for a text they can follow. If you are working on early decoding skills, you may select a text with some decodable words to allow children the chance to practice decoding with your support.
- Select a text that relates to other content (a poem about trees may extend children's knowledge about plants) or interests. Shared reading can be beneficial for foundational skills while still being "real" reading and supporting comprehension.

Setup

- Display the text so that all children can see it.
- Give an authentic purpose for the activity, such as connecting to content or enjoying a poem or song.
- Consider using digital texts, even those with extra features. Some research suggests that using digital rather than print-based texts during shared reading is more beneficial, especially for children who have less knowledge about books and letters (Rvachew et al., 2017; Shamir & Shlafer, 2011).

Timing

- Feel empowered to do shared reading at any time that meets the needs of your students. Research suggests it can be effective at many points in the day (Eldredge et al., 1996).

	BASIC THREE-READ SHARED READING PROTOCOL	
Day/Read	**Steps**	**Sample Dialogue**
Day 1/ Read 1	• Introduce the text: title, author, illustrator, topic, and connection or purpose. • Invite children to make predictions or connect the title/topic to prior knowledge. • Introduce the print concept explicitly (as needed). • Read the text with adult fluency, tracking print as you go. • Point out the print concept. Ask questions about the target print concept. Ask children to help identify all instances of the concept. • Close or move on to Read 2.	"Children, today we are going to read a riddle about an animal. This riddle will tell us some information about an animal, and we will use our knowledge of animal features from science to try to figure out what animal the riddle is about!" "This is a *comma*. We use commas for several reasons. In this text, the comma is used to separate words in a list. When there are three or more things in a list, we put a comma after each item, even when we're also including *and*. This lets the reader identify each thing or phrase in a list. When we see a comma, we often take a little pause in our reading." "What did I do when I got to the comma? Why is there a comma?"
Day 2/ Read 2	• Reintroduce the text as necessary. • Invite children to join you in reading certain parts. You can invite them to join in: the final word of a phrase (especially helpful in poems), decodable words, or words/phrases related to the target print concept. • Read the text with adult fluency, tracking print as you go. • Ask questions about the print concept. • Call children's attention to something else about the text, such as a known sound-spelling relationship, a previously learned print concept, a high-frequency word, etc. • Close or move on to Read 3.	"We just highlighted all the lists. When we get to a list, I want you to join me. Remember, we will take a quick pause when we read a comma." "I noticed this text has a lot of punctuation. We already found the commas. What other punctuation can we see? What does it tell us?"

BASIC THREE-READ SHARED READING PROTOCOL

Day/Read	Steps	Sample Dialogue
Day 3/ Read 3	• Reintroduce the text as necessary. • Invite children to join you in reading the entire text. • Read the text with adult fluency, tracking print as you go. You may also invite a student to track print. • Ask questions about the target print concept. • Ask children comprehension questions related to content or interest. • Close by reminding children about how they used the target print concept. Invite them to notice or use this print concept at other times of day. If possible, allow them to reread the text later in the day on their own or read it aloud with a partner.	"What animal was the riddle about? How do you know?" "Did you like this text? Why or why not?"

(Protocol based on Eldredge et al., 1996; Honchell & Schulz, 2012; Lefebvre et al., 2011)

As I mentioned, shared reading can be used to support almost all foundational skills, not just print concepts. For example, you can use the same structure in shared reading and focus on sound-spelling relationships by:

- Picking a text or writing a text with many instances of the target sound-spelling relationship. It is okay to pick beloved poems, nursery rhymes, songs, or excerpts from books.

- Reminding children about the sound-spelling relationship before reading. "*Ai* can spell the long-*a* sound, such as in the word *pail*."

- Asking questions directly about words with the sound-spelling relationship instead of or in addition to print concepts. "Who can find a word with the long-*a* sound in the middle? Who can find a word with the spelling *ai*? Let's read the word."

- After reading, ask children to extend their sound-spelling knowledge. "We read a bunch of words with the long-*a* sound spelled *ai*. If we spell *pail p-a-i-l*, how do you think we spell *sail*? Spell it on your whiteboard."

If you adjust your shared reading to fit the needs of your students, you can use this basic protocol to support children's development in oral language, print concepts, alphabet knowledge, sound-spelling relationships, decoding, and, indeed, even in chunking.

Bringing It Together

Print knowledge is essential for reading success. It allows children to navigate and access our written language. Supporting children's print concept knowledge is a major part of reading activities in preschool and early kindergarten. Children cannot decode words without first being able to identify words as meaningful. As children become readers, continue to support their understandings of more advanced print concepts like graphics and digital features.

Do It Tomorrow!

Ready to try this shared reading protocol? Go ahead and give it a shot tomorrow.

Worried it won't be perfect? Keep these two points in mind:

- Even if your shared reading isn't perfect, doing them often will positively impact children's print knowledge (Mol et al., 2009), especially if you focus on asking questions to give children the chance to talk.

- Shared reading can be done very quickly. Most shared reading protocols validated in research (like the one on pages 59–60) take less than 15 minutes.

Keep in mind, print concepts are one element of getting children to be decoders. Purposefully target children's print concept knowledge, especially within real reading contexts. As they strengthen their understanding of print, they'll be better equipped to find words to decode and navigate texts.

CHAPTER 5

Element Three:
PHONEMIC AWARENESS

I recently had the honor of visiting Garrison Elementary School in Washington, D.C. Among many recent efforts to improve their early reading instruction, the educators in this building engage in cross-grade, needs-based phonemic awareness work. They've carefully adapted resources to fit their students' unique strengths and needs. Children move through a purposeful, developmentally appropriate progression of phonemic awareness that allows them to gain control over phonemes. Directly following this work, children and teachers turn to reading and spelling those sounds with letters and letter combinations in phonics. This limited (it takes just a few minutes a day) but purposeful phonemic awareness work, directly tied to letters, shows up in reading and spelling across the grades. Children and teachers are thriving.

What Is Phonemic Awareness and Why Is It Important?

Sometimes overshadowed by phonics instruction or overlooked in favor of rhyming games and activities, phonemic awareness is undoubtedly one of the most important elements for decoding. It is the ability to hear and manipulate phonemes, or the smallest sounds in language. Phonemic awareness is a very specific component of phonological awareness, the ability to hear and manipulate sounds in language.

What Is Phonological Awareness and How Is it Different From Phonemic Awareness?

Before we focus on phonemic awareness, it's important to understand the overarching pie of phonological awareness. Phonological awareness includes awareness of very large parts of oral language, such as words and syllables, as well as smaller parts, like onsets (beginning sound of words; /c/ in *cat*) and rimes (part of word after the beginning sound; /at/ in *cat*). It also includes phonemic awareness, the focus of this chapter. As a skill, phonological awareness, including phonemic awareness, is purely oral.

Phonological Awareness

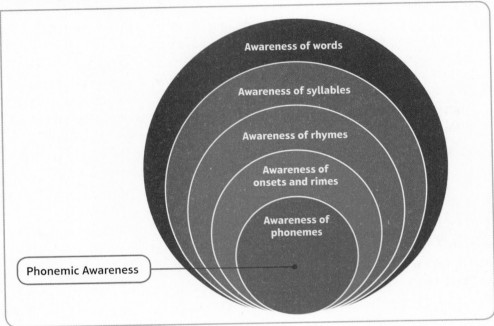

Most of the time, we think about the developmental phonemic awareness in the context of phonological awareness. Generally, phonological awareness develops from larger to smaller units of language, from the beginnings and ends of words to the middle, and from hearing to manipulating parts of words.

Development of Phonological Awareness

Words → Syllables → Rhyming → Onset and rime → Phonemes

Beginning of word → End of word → Middle of word

Hearing → Generating → Isolating → Blending → Segmenting → Manipulating

Our understanding of the development of phonological awareness influences instruction. Looking at this developmental progression, we often think we need to teach syllable awareness, rhyming, and onset-rime awareness before worrying about phonemes. This is reflected in policy, like the Common Core State Standards, and in curricula. At present, however, it is clear that:

- The most important part of phonological awareness for reading and writing is phonemic awareness (NELP, 2008; NICHD, 2000).
- Phonemic awareness might require more explicit instruction than other phonological awareness skills (Rehfeld, 2021).
- Phonemic awareness can be taught to very young children without first teaching phonological awareness (e.g., Becker & Sylvan, 2021).

For these reasons, we will now turn our focus to phonemic awareness.

The Importance of Phonemic Awareness

Trying to help a kindergartner connect a letter form with a sound? Phonemic awareness has a role! Trying to help first graders spell *drop* rather than *jop* or *jrop* or *dop* or *rop*? They need phonemic awareness! Readers cannot map a phoneme (or sound) to a spelling if they cannot hear and manipulate that phoneme. Phonemic awareness is, in many ways, the linchpin for both reading and spelling.

We know from research that overemphasizing this larger progression of phonological awareness might not actually focus us on what really matters for instruction in reading: phonemic awareness. Within phonemic awareness, the two most critical skills for reading and spelling are blending and segmenting (Brown et al., 2021; Ehri, 2014, 2020; NELP, 2008; NRP, 2000).

Phonemic awareness is one of the most robust predictors for future reading success. Here's what just some of the research says:

- Phonemic awareness predicts later decoding abilities and reading comprehension (Caravolas et al., 2019; Clayton et al., 2020).
- Many reading problems, including dyslexia, can be traced, at least in part, to a deficit in phonemic awareness (NELP, 2008; NICHD, 2000; Schaars et al., 2017).

Why is phonemic awareness so key to decoding and other reading skills? Without the ability to discriminate phonemes, mapping phonemes and graphemes isn't just difficult, it is impossible. Luckily, most very young children naturally develop a sensitivity to phonemes (Kenner et al., 2017). However, to ensure and accelerate their phonemic awareness skills, explicit instruction is essential—and can likely prevent some reading difficulties (e.g., Rehfeld, 2021).

As critical as it is to focus on phonemic awareness early in reading instruction, however, it is just as critical to know that phonemic awareness grows reciprocally along with other reading skills (Clayton et al., 2019; Nation & Hulme, 2011; Perfetti et al., 1987). Children do not need to have "mastered" phonemic awareness before they start to learn the alphabet or learn to read some words.

As children learn the alphabet, they need to have basic phonemic awareness skills. Some children will come into your classroom with those skills and others will not and, therefore, will need to be taught them, along with your alphabet instruction. Those skills include:

- Hearing individual phonemes: A child must be able to hear /t/ to associate it with the letter *t*.
- Generating individual phonemes: A child must be able to say /t/ to associate it with the letter *t*.

PHONEMIC AWARENESS SKILL DEVELOPMENT
This is an overlapping sequence of skills, from easy (for most children) to more challenging.

Skill	Definition
Hearing	Hearing and distinguishing individual phonemes in isolation, sometimes referred to as "matching" EXAMPLE: /m/ and /n/ are two different sounds
Generating	Saying individual phonemes EXAMPLE: Saying the sound /t/
Isolating	Hearing and identifying individual phonemes in words EXAMPLE: *bed* starts with /b/
Blending	Putting individual phonemes together to say a word EXAMPLE: The sounds /d/ /o/ /g/ make the word *dog*
Segmenting	Separating each individual phoneme in a word EXAMPLE: Hearing the sounds /c/ /a/ /t/ in the word *cat*
Manipulating	Adding, deleting, or substituting individual phonemes in words EXAMPLE: Changing the medial vowel changes *hot* to *hat*

Phonemic awareness instruction should match students' reading and spelling development, moving from easier to harder tasks and moving from exclusively oral tasks to including letters (NELP, 2008; NRP, 2000). It should also move rapidly from exclusively oral tasks to including letters (see the box below). As children begin to become fluent with the alphabet and individual phonemes, have them work on isolating the phonemes in one-syllable words, which will enable them to accurately spell each phoneme they hear, and read each phoneme they see represented in print. Before or when children start spelling and reading words, they should be:

- Isolating phonemes in two- and three-sound words (such as *at* /a/ /t/ and *pan* /p/ /a/ /n/) beginning with initial sound, then final sound, and then medial sound.
- Blending and segmenting two- and three-sound words. More on this in the next section.

As children start becoming readers, they can also work on the final phonemic awareness skill: manipulation, which involves swapping parts of words to create new words. For example, "What word do I get if I change the /d/ to /l/ in *dog*?" Some research suggests this skill does not develop until children are already reading, so it does not need to be a major focus in the early stage of instruction. However, as children start to become readers, they should be using letters and phonemes simultaneously to demonstrate phonemic awareness skills, while working on solidifying their understanding of how letters and spellings represent sounds.

> **Is "Oral Only" a Red Herring?**
>
> Once children are working with letters, they are better served by focusing on phonemic awareness practice that includes letters (NELP, 2008; NRP, 2000). Another way to say this is: Once children know some sound-spelling relationships, they should mostly be working with letters and sounds *together* (Clemens et al., 2021). Therefore, phonemic awareness practice should often include:
>
> - Isolating the first sound in a spoken word (*man* /m/) and then spelling the sound (m).
> - Blending sounds to read words (seeing *tag* and saying /t/ /a/ /g/).
> - Segmenting sounds to spell words (hearing a word and writing a spelling for each sound).
> - Manipulating sounds and spellings. (Write the word *mug*. Change the last sound to make it *mud*. What letter did you change?)

Blending and Segmenting Are Key

The most critical subskills of phonemic awareness are blending (/l/ /a/ /p/ becomes *lap*) and segmenting (*lap* becomes /l/ /a/ /p/) because they are essential prerequisites for decoding and encoding (spelling). Children cannot apply sound-spelling knowledge to a word if they can say the sounds only in isolation; they need to be able to blend them together. Segmenting and blending abilities are better at predicting later reading achievement than rhyming abilities (Hatcher & Hulme, 1999; Hatcher et al., 2004; Muter et al., 1998; Nation & Hulme, 1997). Additionally, children who can segment and blend words orally have better decoding skills. Lastly, children who are struggling with decoding and spelling also have deficits in phonemic awareness (Spear-Swerling, 2016). Blending and segmenting are necessary for reading and writing words. Even adults may benefit from them when they encounter unfamiliar words.

Principles of Great Phonemic Awareness Instruction

It's not enough to hope phonemic awareness skills develop naturally. In fact, it's not even enough for us to just model them. We need to support children's learning of phonemic awareness skills in a reasonable developmental progression and give them plenty of opportunities to practice those skills. Like all foundational skills, I suggest following these four principles for great instruction.

1 Explicitly and Systematically Address Phonemic Awareness

Phonemic awareness lends itself to explicit, systematic instruction because of its clear developmental progression. Align your phonemic awareness instruction with your phonics instruction for the best outcomes (NRP, 2000). For example, teach children how to isolate initial sounds in words while you teach them the alphabet to help them match sounds to letters. Teach them phonemic manipulation when you teach consonant blends so they can compare minimal pairs (i.e., two words that vary by one letter or sound, such as *clap* and *cap*) to focus in on the consonant blend (e.g., *cl*) (Tuan, 2010).

2 Follow an Efficient and Effective Routine, Connecting Phonemic Awareness to Alphabet Letters as Soon as Children Are Able

Phonemic awareness instruction should never take up a substantial amount of time in your day. I'm serious. You do not need to overdo it. There is no evidence that children need isolated oral phoneme work for an extended time each day. In fact, the National Reading Panel recommendations amount to 15 hours total for the whole school year (2000). That means about five minutes per day for 180 days. As soon as children can work with letters, it is important to add those letters into your phonemic awareness instruction, even if it seems counterintuitive. Of course, doing that makes phonemic awareness more relevant to real reading.

3 Respond to Specific Needs of Children Based on Assessment Results. But Don't Expect Mastery too Early

Supplemental K–2 phonemic awareness interventions support reading and have a lasting effect (Suggate, 2016). If you notice a child struggling with phonemic awareness, give him or her opportunities for practice. Try not to overdiagnose, though. As explained earlier, phonemic awareness grows along with reading, so if a child isn't mastering phonemic awareness before he or she starts reading, do not panic.

It's quick and easy to assess phonemic awareness. You can access a free, research-based assessment from the Mountain Shadows Assessment (edpsychassociates.com/Watkins3.html). You can also carry out your own informal assessment by asking questions such as the ones on the following page, depending on your children's progress. These questions can help you decide which children need additional support.

> *Phonemic awareness instruction should never take up a substantial amount of time in your day…. There is no evidence that children need isolated oral phoneme work for an extended time each day.*

INFORMAL ASSESSMENT QUESTIONS	
Skill	**Sample Questions**
Hearing	"Is /s/ the same sound as /b/?"
Isolating	Initial Sound: "What sound do you hear first in the word *bam*?" Final Sound: "What sound do you hear last in the word *bam*?" Medial Sound: "What sound do you hear in the middle of the word *bam*?"
Blending	"What word is this: /f/ /i/ /n/?"
Segmenting	"Say all the sounds in the word *fin*."
Manipulating	"What word do you get if you delete the /l/ sound from the word *clap*?"

4 Support Phonemic Awareness With Phonics and in Real Reading Contexts

As soon as children have gained some proficiency with a few letter-sound pairings during phonemic awareness instruction (current research suggests about eight pairings, including some vowels), they can work on blending and segmenting both phonemes and letters—in other words, phonics and decoding (Ehri, 2020). Don't wait for a magical moment to introduce letters into your phonemic awareness routines, in other words. Phonemic awareness and alphabet knowledge operate together to enhance early reading (Brady, 2021).

In preschool and early kindergarten, before children are blending and segmenting words, introduce those skills during read-aloud by modeling how to decode words, sing songs that contain rhythmic phonemes instead of rhymes, and play word games that emphasize sounds, such as Picnic: "We're going on a picnic and we can each bring one thing that starts with the sound /p/."

Fewer Rhymes, More Phonemes

You've probably noticed that I haven't talked much about rhyming. Rhyming, a component of phonological awareness often focused on in preschool and kindergarten, is not needed to decode or spell. (For example, a child can learn to read the word *orange* even though it does not rhyme with any other word in English.) We do not need to spend lots of time practicing rhyming to support children's word reading. Phonemic awareness, on the other hand, most certainly is critical to reading.

A few recent studies point to why you can probably skip rhyming and go straight to phonemic awareness. First, as I stated earlier, children start noticing and hearing phonemes as toddlers (Kenner et al., 2017). This suggests they do not have to first rhyme to then hear phonemes. Second, teaching phonemic awareness as early as preschool is effective (e.g., Becker & Sylvan, 2021). If the purpose of your instruction is giving children the keys to decoding, then focus on building skills that prepare them for decoding: segmenting and blending.

An Effective and Efficient Routine for Phonemic Awareness Instruction

Phonemic awareness routines should be oral, short, and intense. Use explicit instruction, modeling, and guided practice to give children the chance to quickly practice a specific aspect of phonemic awareness. Consider including manipulatives or magnetic letters to make your routines more concrete and ensure that children are working with letters and sounds as soon as possible.

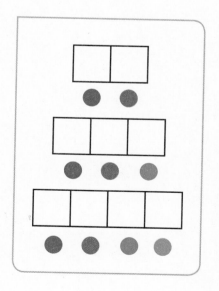

Elkonin boxes, which are sometimes called sound boxes or word boxes (Elkonin, 1963; Keesey et al., 2015; Schacter & Jo, 2005), are a great tool for building phonemic awareness. On the next page is a quick routine that you can use with the whole class, small groups, or individuals to support phonemic awareness, using Elkonin boxes, like the ones to the right.

ROUTINE FOR PHONEMIC AWARENESS INSTRUCTION	
Instruct and Model	Pick one aspect of phonemic awareness based on your scope and sequence. This example demonstrates three-sound blending.
	"We can put together sounds to make words. When we put sounds together, we slide through them, connecting each sound. I can use the boxes and my coin (or other manipulative) to help me slide through each sound. Watch me slide through the sounds /s/ /a/ /t/."
	Put a coin on the first box and say /s/. Hold the sound as you move to the second box and say /a/. Hold the sound as you move to the third box and say /t/. Move the coin back to the first box and say all the sounds together as you quickly run the coin across the boxes.
	"This word is *sat!*"
Together	Give each child three boxes and a coin. Practice with children for 3 to 5 words.
Practice	Say three sounds, such as /r/ /a/ /p/. Have children whisper to themselves as they slide across sounds. Have children tell their partner the word. If children are spelling, have children write the word on a paper to check their blending and segmenting. Repeat with 5 to 8 words.
Close	Ideally, move into a lesson on sound-spelling relationships or reading of a decodable text so that children can directly apply their knowledge.
	"We listen for and slide through sounds in words so that we are able to read and write words!"

(Based on Keesey et al., 2015)

You can add letters (magnetic letters, letter cards, foam letters) to Elkonin boxes using the same routine as above. Be sure to preplan the words you will have children work with. Give children around six letters to manipulate at a time. Children then place the letters into the corresponding boxes, effectively spelling the word. You can also use this procedure with just one sound at a time: "We're listening for the first sound in the word *mop*. Point to the first box as you say the first sound and then slide across as you finish the word: *mmmop*. Now, put the letter that makes the first sound in the first box!"

Start With Continuous Sounds

Starting by having children segment and blend consonant-vowel-consonant (CVC) words that begin with continuous sounds leads to stronger word-reading outcomes (Gonzalez-Frey & Ehri, 2021). Some options include words that begin with *m, s, f, l, r, n, v,* and *z*. For example, for the word *sat,* you might say,

> *I can say all the sounds in this word by saying it very slowly. Listen to me say all the sounds in the word sat. SSSSSaaaaaaat. Now, watch as I pull my coin across the sound boxes to say each sound again, pulling across the box that matches the sound. SSSSSaaaaaaat. Now, you try!*

You never need to segment the word fully. This may help children because when we keep the sounds connected, we don't unintentionally change the sound or add a *schwa* to individual sounds (an unstressed vowel sound; you can hear it at the beginning of words like *about* and *along* and you can hear it after many stop sounds if you don't clip the sound: For example, *puh* instead of /p/). Once children show they can segment CVC words with continuous sounds, move onto more traditional segmenting with stop sounds (such as *pat*).

Bringing It Together

Although phonemic awareness is a critical element of decoding, it alone does not ensure that children will learn to decode. They must also know sound-spelling correspondences. Certainly, phonemic segmentation and blending may *facilitate* decoding, but without sound-spelling knowledge, they are insufficient. Engage primary students in short, and ideally, daily routines that connect phonemic awareness to phonics instruction and that add letters to the target sounds so that what students are learning is more directly applicable to reading and writing.

CHAPTER 6

Element Four:
ALPHABET KNOWLEDGE

I n my first year of teaching, I used a scripted phonics curriculum that had me teach the alphabet in 26 days, one letter a day. I had no clue whether that was a reasonable approach or not, so I just went with it. At the end of the unit, my kindergartners could identify, on average, 98 percent of lower- and uppercase letters by name, form, and sound.

You might be thinking, "Sure, but how many of those kids came in with that knowledge already?" Honestly, I don't remember the exact number, but some did. However, for the sake of this discussion, the exact number doesn't matter. Why? Because you, too, will undoubtedly have children who come to your classroom already knowing the alphabet, who will not be served by slow alphabet instruction. As for the children who come to your classroom without any alphabet knowledge, it turns out they may benefit the most from accelerated instruction (Sunde et al., 2020). Not only will they get exposure to the alphabet quickly so they can begin reading and writing, but you will be able to identify and address alphabet-knowledge needs earlier. Everybody wins!

What Is Alphabet Knowledge and Why Is It Important?

Alphabet knowledge, the first step in understanding sound-spelling relationships, consists of knowing the name, form, and common sound(s) for each letter in the alphabet—more specifically, knowing the most common sound for each consonant and sounds for short vowels. It is closely related to the alphabetic principle, defined as "the understanding that language is made up of discrete sounds and that letters represent those sounds in a systematic way" (Huang et al., 2014, p. 182). The alphabetic principle is a crucial understanding for beginning readers to grasp. Without it, they are unlikely to develop successful word-reading skills (Stanovich, 2009). One of the first concepts for children to understand is that printed letters represent sounds.

The alphabetic principle is a crucial understanding for beginning readers to grasp. Without it, they are unlikely to develop successful word-reading skills.

Alphabet knowledge is one of the strongest predictors of later achievement in reading (e.g., Leppanen et al., 2008; NELP, 2008). Here's what research says:

1. **Letter-name knowledge** (i.e., knowing the name of a letter when presented with the form) is consistently found to be a predictor of long-term success in learning to read (Hammill, 2004; Share et al., 1984).

2. **Letter-sound knowledge** (i.e., knowing the sound[s] a letter makes) in the first year of reading instruction is a predictor of word-reading and reading growth across that year (Clayton et al., 2020), as well as a predictor of decoding and comprehension in the following years (Caravolas et al., 2019).

What Should I Teach First: Letter Names or Sounds?

You might hear colleagues saying we don't need to teach the names of letters as much as we need to teach their sounds. They might point out that names are not always helpful because those names don't always match the sounds the letters spell. For example, the letter name *f* starts with the short-*e* sound. They might insist that we teach sounds first because that's what children need to use to decode. Research has investigated this question and has some answers for us:

1. In a meta-analysis of alphabet studies, Piasta and Wagner (2010) found that teaching alphabet names and sounds together led to the best outcomes. More recently, Roberts and colleagues (2018) found that learning letter sounds and names at the same time led to effective learning of names and sounds.

2. Other studies indicate that letter-name knowledge can help children learn letter sounds because many letter names contain a common and, therefore, dependable sound (e.g., Share, 2004; Treiman et al., 1998), for example:

   - The five vowel-letter names (*a, e, i, o, u*) make the long sounds.
   - Consonant names with a common sound first: *b, d, j, k, p, t, v, z*
   - Consonant names with a common sound last: *f, l, m, n, r, s, x*
   - Consonant names with a slightly less common sound first: *c, g*
   - Consonant names with no association to the sound: *h, q, w, y*

3. Most research-tested alphabet protocols include both names and sounds— and they positively impact children's reading (e.g., Jones et al., 2013; Roberts et al., 2018).

The big takeaway: It is likely best to teach letter names and sounds simultaneously (Piasta et al., 2010; Roberts, 2021).

Relatedly, producing a letter's form (handwriting) is likely to fuel children's literacy development. Though more research is needed, at least one study shows that early handwriting skills predict spelling development (Pritchard et al., 2021). Because spelling and reading are interconnected, handwriting could potentially support early reading. Another study found that alphabet instruction with an emphasis on forming letters might build alphabet knowledge specifically for multilingual learners (Roberts et al., 2019).

Alphabet knowledge is an essential element in decoding because it is the start of children's journeys to an understanding of written English language. Even just knowing letters exist is pivotal in understanding all sound-spelling relationships, engaging in conversations about written language, and recognizing and writing letter forms. The goal of teaching the alphabet is for children to be able to match letter forms automatically and accurately to their names and sounds. That goal should guide your instructional choices.

Principles of Great Alphabet Instruction

Taking what we know from research and practice, here are four instructional principles for building alphabet knowledge.

1 Explicitly and Systematically Address Alphabet Knowledge

Just like all foundational skills instruction, it's best to teach the alphabet in a systematic and explicit way. There is not a perfect scope and sequence for the alphabet, but you can ensure you have a good one.

A good alphabet scope and sequence contains a lot of information about letter names, sounds, and forms. Ideally, letters that are too similar shouldn't be taught at the same time. For example, the letters *m* and *n* shouldn't be taught back-to-back because they are easily confused. Other easily confused letters include those with letter forms that share specific distinctive features, such as E/F, M/N/W, P/R, b/d/p/q, m/n/u. When teaching these letters, emphasize the features that distinguish the letters (Jones et al., 2013).

Another uncommon, but incredibly important, feature of a good alphabet scope and sequence is one that encourages devoting more time to harder-to-learn letters. You do not need to spend the same amount of time on each letter. From research, we know the letters that are likely to be the hardest for children to learn (Jones et al., 2013):

- letters from the middle of the alphabet (*l, m, n, o, p*)
- letters that are visually or phonologically similar (e.g., *b, d* and *c, k*)
- letters with mismatched sounds and names (see above)
- infrequent letters (*w, x, z, j, q, y*)

Jones and colleagues (2013) suggest cycles of alphabet instruction in which you devote more time to hard-to-learn letters to ensure children get adequate exposure to them, instead of devoting the same amount of time to every letter.

Finally, introduce letters rapidly. Check out the instructional swap on page 84 to see how rapidly and find an example scope and sequence.

2 Follow an Efficient and Effective Routine

Alphabet instruction doesn't need to take a lot of time, as the instructional swap on page 84 proves. Many research-tested routines take under 15 minutes. This is possible by focusing on what really matters in alphabet instruction and cutting the fluff.

Remember that the purpose of alphabet instruction is to ensure children can automatically and accurately match letter forms to sounds and names. Thus, instruction should mostly be about matching forms, sounds, and names.

Certain instructional decisions make a difference for children learning the alphabet (Jones et al., 2013; Roberts, 2021; Roberts et al., 2018, 2019, 2020). For example, clear, concise, and stable routines are best. Decontextualized instruction works better than instruction inside stories and other types of texts. The best alphabet instruction focuses just on the letter forms (such as a single letter on a card) paired with the names and sounds. Show children the letter, say its sound and name, and have the children say its sound and name repeatedly. Letter cards support letter name-sound-form associations best when they include embedded picture clues (i.e., objects that begin with the target phoneme) (Shmidman & Ehri, 2010). See the next page for two examples with the letter *B*.

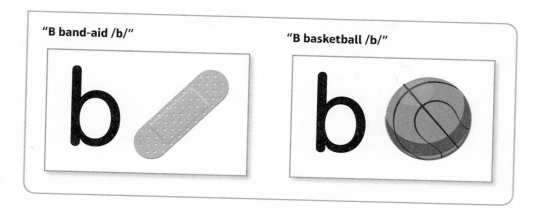

"B band-aid /b/" "B basketball /b/"

You might think I'm advocating "skill-and-drill." But I'm not. It might surprise you—it surprised me!—that children might be *more* engaged in this type of instruction than a more holistic alphabet-learning experience. Roberts and colleagues (2020) compared decontextualized alphabet instruction to alphabet instruction within stories and found that children were more participatory and attentive, and appeared happier, during the former. In an additional study, the same team (2019) found that children's self-reported motivation to learn increased after decontextualized alphabet instruction. As counterintuitive as that may seem, these are important findings to consider. They remind us that motivation and engagement in learning are not always related to what we adults think will excite children. Straightforward decontextualized instruction is sometimes the more motivating and engaging choice to teach a particular skill.

> *Motivation and engagement in learning are not always related to what we adults think will excite children. Straightforward, decontextualized instruction is sometimes the more motivating and engaging choice to teach a particular skill.*

3 Respond to the Specific Needs of Children Based on Assessment

One of the biggest advantages to introducing the alphabet quickly is that it gives you more time to respond to specific needs. The best way to determine those needs is through ongoing progress monitoring and then addressing children's challenges through needs-based instruction. I suggest beginning this effort in earnest after you introduce the entire alphabet through whole-class instruction.

You don't need anything fancy for a standard alphabet assessment. You can even create your own. Show each child one letter at a time and ask, "What is this letter's name?" If the child answers correctly, go on to ask, "What sound does it make?" Be sure to take notes. You should assess children on both upper- and lowercase letters. Then create small groups based on patterns you observe.

You might have a group that's mastered names, but not sounds. Children in that group may best be served by first reviewing consonant names with a common sound first—such as *b, d, j, k, p, t, v,* and *z*—to help them use their knowledge of names to learn sounds. Or you might form a group of children who confuse visually similar letters, like *b* and *d*, and might be best served by repeated interaction with and comparison of those letters and, as some research suggests, opportunities to write those letters (Zemlock et al., 2018).

Beware District Screeners and Computer-Based Assessments

Alphabet knowledge is a constrained skill. You either know a letter's name, form, and common sound or you do not. Knowing one letter does not predict whether you know another letter. Many assessments designed for large-scale use (most computerized assessments fit into this category) do not actually assess children on all 26 letters. They might estimate a child's alphabet knowledge based on nine letters to keep the assessment short and sweet. This might be okay for identifying potential at-risk readers or estimating an entire district's literacy, but this is not okay for instruction. It is critical that you (or another member of your school's staff) know exactly what each child in your classroom knows about all the alphabet letters. This is the only way to appropriately respond to their specific alphabet needs.

4 Support Alphabet Knowledge With Other Foundational Skills and in Real Reading Contexts

Though the alphabet is best learned through decontextualized instruction (see above), we can't stop there. Just like all foundational skills, alphabet knowledge isn't very useful if children don't do anything with it. Children need to apply what they learn in context.

One way to do that is to embed references to the alphabet when teaching other aspects of your foundational skills instruction:

- **If you're doing a shared reading focused on print concepts,** for example, an alliterative text containing words with a target letter, point out that target letter in a couple of places, and then ask the children to find it during the shared reading and say its name and sound.

- **If you're giving a phonemic awareness lesson,** for example, as soon as children are working with letters, include those letters in that lesson. This is easiest if your alphabet scope and sequence pairs well with your phonemic awareness instruction. For example, if you are teaching the letter *s*, have children isolate the initial sound in words such as *sun* and *sad*. After working with words orally, ask children questions such as, "What letter spells /s/?" to help them begin to bridge the gaps between alphabet knowledge, phonemic awareness, reading, and spelling.

Teach Like a Hare, Not a Tortoise!

Of all the principles for great alphabet instruction, the most important one is to speed it up, in terms of how you move through your scope and sequence and your daily routine.

Two recent studies illuminate how quickly in kindergarten you should introduce the alphabet. Sunde and colleagues (2020) found that children who were in classes in which the teacher introduced the entire alphabet within about the first three months of the school year performed better on measures of letter-sound knowledge, word decoding, and high-frequency word reading at the year's end than children who were in classes in which the teacher introduced the alphabet more gradually. Furthermore, children in those fast-paced classrooms with the lowest knowledge at the start of the year benefited the most by the end of the year. Vadasy and Sanders (2021) attempted to determine how fast is fast enough. They found that kindergartners and first graders (including multilingual learners) learning three letter-sound correspondences a week outperformed peers in slower paced instruction in alphabet knowledge, decoding, and spelling.

Of all the principles for great alphabet instruction, the most important one is to speed it up, in terms of how you move through your scope and sequence and your daily routine.

Given that information, I suggest introducing at least three letters a week and, based on assessments, returning to hard-to-learn letters (Jones et al., 2013) as needed. As children begin to read regular consonant-vowel-consonant (CVC) words toward the end of your alphabet instruction and beyond it, continue to review letter-sound correspondences to ensure they're committed to memory. If you are teaching preschool, I do recommend a slower pace; however, the instructional routine on page 86 is based on research with both preschoolers and kindergarteners, so it can be used in either context.

A POSSIBLE SCOPE AND SEQUENCE FOR INTRODUCING LETTERS			
Week	**Alphabet Letters**	**Week**	**Alphabet Letters**
1	m, t, a	10	If needed, revisit infrequent letters: w, x, z, j, q, y
2	b, s, n	11	If needed, revisit letters with mismatched sounds and names: h, q, w, y, c, g, s
3	p, e, r		
4	d, l, c		
5	i, f, k	12	If needed, revisit the middle of the alphabet: l, m, n, o, p
6	j, v, o	13	If needed, revisit visually similar letters: E/F, M/N/W, P/R, b/d/p/q, m/n/u
7	u, g, h		
8	v, z, x	14	If needed, revisit vowels
9	w, y	15	If needed, revisit any letters

An Effective and Efficient Routine for Alphabet Instruction

Alphabet lessons themselves should also be fast. As I explained in the earlier section called "Use an efficient (under 15 minutes) and effective (research-proven) routine," there is no need to spend an hour a day on the alphabet. By using the most effective routines and focusing on the purpose of alphabet learning, you can teach more expediently. Try this 10-minute routine to teach each letter. It is best suited for small group. However, it works with the whole class when the children sit on the carpet in a circle. Give each child a whiteboard (for formation) and letter cards or tiles of previously learned letters (for review and find). Use turn-and-talks or choral responses to ensure all children are participating and learning and check each child's writing on the whiteboard.

ROUTINE FOR ALPHABET INSTRUCTION	
Review	Show letter cards for previous learned letters. "What letter? What sound does it spell?" Have children repeat the correct answer.
Name and Say	Show a letter card. "This is our new letter, (name) (sound). Say ___." "(name) spells (sound) like at the start of (target word/embedded picture). Repeat after me." "This is the uppercase letter ___. Say ___." "This is the lowercase letter ___. Say ___." Have children repeat the sound at least three times.
Find and Read	Show a mix of letters. Have children find the target letter and say the name and sound using prompts like, "Find the letter that spells the sound ___ and say its sound. Find the letter named ___ and say its sound." Show a print-salient text or alphabet book. Have children find the target letter and say the name and sound.
Form	Model formation of an upper- and lowercase letter. Have children write or trace the letter as they say the sound. Have children write the letter as they say the sound three times with prompts like, "Write the letter that spells the sound ___ and say its sound. Write the letter named___ and say its sound."
Close	Show a letter card. "This is the letter (name) (sound). Say ___." "(name) spells (sound) like at the start of (target word/embedded picture). Repeat after me."

(Protocol based on Jones et al., 2013; Roberts et al., 2018, 2019, 2020)

What About Articulation? Mouth Movements? Sound Walls?

For some children, it may be helpful to add articulation instruction to your alphabet instruction. This can sound like: "When I say the sound ___, I (describe mouth and tongue position)." This can also include mirrors for children to look at their own mouths.

Some research (Boyer & Ehri, 2011) suggests articulation instruction is helpful for segmenting, spelling, and word reading. Other research (Roberts et al., 2019) finds that articulation instruction within alphabet instruction is most helpful for multilingual learners but isn't particularly helpful for other children. To my knowledge, there is no evidence that articulation instruction harms children. As I write this, there are no studies about sound walls (wall displays that show the mouth movement and sound associated with a letter), so research cannot tell us if these support, harm, or do nothing for children. Thus, at present, we do not have a perfect clear-cut answer on this from research.

I suggest using your professional judgment and knowledge about your students. If you teach lots of multilingual learners, it is likely a good idea to include articulation instruction from Day 1. If you teach lots of monolingual English speakers, you might prefer to carefully observe children and add in articulation instruction as needed or include it instead in your phonemic awareness instruction (as Boyer & Ehri, 2011). You might decide to try a sound wall and see if it supports your children, or you might decide to wait until more information is available. In my eyes, all those choices are valid as long as you continue to monitor students' progress to ensure your choice is working for them.

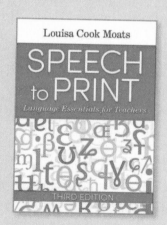

For more on articulation and our language system, I suggest reading *Speech to Print: Language Essentials for Teachers*, *Third Edition*, by Louisa Cook Moats.

Bringing It Together

Alphabet knowledge is critical for reading and writing. Alphabet knowledge is one of the first steps toward a child's ability to decode and create orthographic maps of words because children realize that letters symbolize sounds and create words. Most children can master the alphabet by the middle of kindergarten with the right instruction.

In addition to the principles and swap on pages 84–87, you can support alphabet learning throughout the day. Try using print-salient texts during read-alouds and pointing out learned letters, reminding children of the name-sound-form correspondence. Point out environmental print around the school on the way to lunch or specials. Model noticing a letter and saying its sound to read, not its name. These small moves, throughout the day, can add up to many more necessary exposures to name-sound-form correspondence, accelerating children's learning.

We're getting closer to decoding! Alphabet knowledge is a just a small step away from getting children to be decoders. Using an efficient, research-proven routine, you can meet our four principles of great foundational skills instruction.

Read-aloud was my absolute favorite time of day as a teacher. I loved picking silly books, beautiful books, books with fascinating new facts to read with my students. I loved sharing a new vocabulary word for my students to try out throughout the day. Imagine my surprise, then, when I asked my kindergartners, "What's the best time of day?" and several responded, with large smiles on their faces, "Phonics!"

What we think is the most joyful isn't always the most joyful for all the children in front of us. That's not to say that those students disliked read-aloud time, just that they loved learning new letters and sounds—and I was more than happy to lean into that!

Do It Tomorrow!

If you have children who need support in alphabet knowledge, you can give faster instruction a try tomorrow. Find 10 spare minutes and pull a small group together to work on one letter.

- If you don't have alphabet cards, you can create some from your computer. I recommend using the Century Gothic font.

- If you don't know what target word to choose, think of a word that begins with your target, but does not begin with a consonant blend. Bonus points if you pick a word that's familiar to your students or special to your school and/or community—for example, if you live in Michigan, you might choose the letter *m* and say, "This is the letter *m*, which spells the sound /m/ like at the start of *Michigan*."

Element Five:
SOUND-SPELLING KNOWLEDGE

Very often we educators equate a quiet classroom with a productive classroom. After all, when children are silent, they're likely engaged in deep thinking. In truth, however, silence during reading time should be viewed as a massive red flag.

When children are learning sound-spelling relationships and applying them, they should be extremely vocal. At that stage in their development, we need to embrace the noise. Children need to hear the sounds to map them to spelling. Next time you release children to literacy centers, stations, or small groups for phonics, don't ask them to work quietly. Say you want to hear them listening for, saying, or spelling sounds. The more practice they have doing that, the more automatically and accurately they will be able to apply sound-spelling knowledge to reading.

What Are Sound-Spelling Relationships and Why Are They Important?

Sound-spelling relationships go by many names, including phoneme-grapheme correspondences, letter-sound relationships, and combinations of those terms. In essence, this chapter is all about instruction in the correspondences between spellings and the sounds they represent. And instruction in mapping spelling to sounds is—drumroll please—phonics! Since the National Reading Panel's (NRP) report (2000), it has been widely accepted that phonics instruction is the most efficient and effective way to teach word reading.

Decades of research tells us that phonics instruction is hugely helpful in developing children's reading and spelling (Henbest & Apel, 2017; NRP, 2000; Torgerson, et al., 2018). Studies targeting specific groups, such as children experiencing poverty, children who are learning English, and children of color, continue to reveal a strong, positive relationship between high-quality phonics and reading (Chu & Chen, 2014; Dessemontet et

Why "Sound-Spelling Relationships"?

You might be wondering why I'm using sound-spelling relationships instead of a different term, such as letter-sound relationships.

First, using "spelling" rather than "letter" reminds us that children need to learn far more than just the letters to break our orthographic code.

Second, it emphasizes that spellings are representations of sounds (or pronunciations) and, therefore, reminds us of the oral aspect of learning to read. Kids need to listen and speak a lot at this early stage in their reading development.

al., 2019; Ehri & Flugman, 2018; Fien et al., 2015). Though there is always more to learn about how to best teach phonics, especially for groups that have been excluded from research in the past, we have strong evidence that explicit, systematic phonics serves young readers well.

Sound-spelling knowledge is necessary for students to become proficient readers (Moats, 2009). I've already pointed out how critical alphabet knowledge is for reading, that children know, for example, that *b* represents /b/ at the start of *bus*. But what about more advanced sound-spelling knowledge, such as knowing *eigh* represents long /i/ in *height*? Children need more than just alphabet knowledge, without question.

Remember that we represent oral phonemes (sounds) with written spellings (letters or combinations of letters). There are 44 phonemes in English and at least 250 ways to spell them (Moats, 2000). For example, the sound in the end of the word *for* (/or/) can be spelled *or* (as in *for*), *our* (as in *four*), *oar* (as in *board*), or *ore* (as in *lore*). This one phoneme (/or/) can be spelled at least four ways. Quite a bit more than just 26 letter-sound relationships!

A proficient reader can instantly recognize between 30,000–70,000 words with those phonemes and spellings. To provide this foundation, it is critical to teach children how to map phonemes to spellings. As children master phonemic awareness, they begin to hear all 44 phonemes and, from there, begin to represent them in print as they attempt to spell them. To read, the reverse is true: They need to see letters and letter combinations, and automatically know which phonemes are represented to read a word accurately.

> **Teaching Children Linguistic Terms**
>
> Do you need to teach children linguistic terms such as *phoneme* or *digraph* or *voiced dental fricative* (/th/ sound)? Probably not. I am not familiar with any studies about teaching these terms to children. I am also familiar with many, many adults and children who can read without knowing these linguistic terms.
>
> Some terms might be helpful to students in categorizing sound-spelling relationships, such as *digraphs*, which are two letters spelling one sound. Outside of that, however, there may not be a benefit to teaching linguistic terms. In fact, too much emphasis on terminology may distract from the much more important work of learning and using sound-spelling relationships.

The Benefits of Self-Teaching

Share's Self-Teaching Hypothesis (1995) says that readers learn word-specific orthography (or spelling) by decoding. In other words, readers learn spellings of new words by decoding them. Then, they integrate that information into memory, saving the spelling for use in reading other words. This is called orthographic learning. But before readers can engage in it, they must have some ability to decode words by knowing how spellings relate to sounds.

"Efficient word identification is directly tied to strong mental representations of words, which include spellings, meanings and pronunciations (Ehri, 2005; Perfetti, 2007). Orthographic learning is the process by which these representations for individual words are acquired" (Share, 2008).

As readers encounter more complex words, however, they are likely to learn some sound-spelling correspondences on their own from repeatedly decoding certain words, using the knowledge they have (Pritchard et al., 2018; Share, 1995). In other words, "the rich get richer." Orthographic knowledge (knowledge of spellings) impacts how successfully a child can self-teach, *and* successful self-teaching impacts orthographic knowledge (Pritchard, 2018; Share, 1999).

It is unlikely that your phonics scope and sequence covers 250 sound-spelling correspondences. It is also unwise to focus our energy on having children memorize all correspondences in their early years of schooling. Some of these sound-spellings correspondences are rare, with a spelling matching to a phoneme in less than 5 percent of written words with that particular phoneme (Hanna et al., 1966). For example, when we hear the sound /short a/, it is almost always spelled *a* (as in *bat*), and it is very rarely spelled *ai* (as in *plaid*). Some of sound-spelling correspondences do not appear in any single-syllable words, so young readers are unlikely to come across them.

In the early elementary years, focus on the highest utility sound-spelling relationships: those that are somewhat stable, and commonly found in single-syllable words (such as *ea* represents /long e/ in words like *bean*) or regular multisyllabic words (such as *le* represents /l/ at the end of words like *bubble*). Children should learn the major sound-spelling correspondences in a reasonable sequence (Buckingham, 2020), which gives them access to English orthography and, when paired with real reading and writing, supports them in self-teaching (Share, 1995).

In later elementary years, build on children's base knowledge of common sound-spelling correspondences to give them access to more advanced English orthography. In this chapter, I focus on the sound-spelling relationships that are most foundational to early reading, which are typically taught in kindergarten through second grade. In Chapter 9, I focus on children's early multisyllabic word-reading needs.

Principles of Great Phonics Instruction

Great phonics instruction begins with you. First and foremost, check your own knowledge of our orthographic system.

- **Do you know the details of sound-spelling generalizations you're going to teach?** For example, *gh* can represent /f/, but not when it's at the beginning of a word. See pages 96 and 97 for some common sound-spelling correspondences.

- **Do you know how to say each phoneme in isolation?** As adults, we don't tend to do this very often and might need a refresher. Most of us add extra sounds to phonemes (we might say *buh* instead of /b/). Bizarre as it sounds, we must take a step back, check our own pronunciations, and practice those sounds in isolation. Grab a friend and practice together. YouTube can be a source for proper sounds if you aren't sure.

VOWEL SOUNDS		
Short and long vowel sounds	**Example**	**Common spellings (most common is on top)**
Short *a*	map	*a* *au, ae, ai*
Long *a*	mane	*a* *a_e, ai, aigh, ay, ea, ei, ey*
Short *e*	men	*e* *ea, ie, ai*
Long *e*	mean	*e* *ee, ea, e_e, ei, ey, i, ie, i_e, y*
Short *i*	pin	*i* *y*
Long *i*	pine	*i_e* *i, ie, igh, ei, eigh, uy, y*
Short *o*	pot	*o*
Long *o*	so	*o* *o_e, oa, oe, ou, ew, ow, ough, eau*
Short *u*	pun	*u* *ou*
Long *u*	cube	*u* *u_e, ue, ew, eau*

CONSONANT SOUNDS		
Common consonant sounds	**Example**	**Most common spellings (most common is top)**
Typical consonant-alphabet sounds	*p* spells /p/	The most common spelling is, luckily, each letter. Exceptions: /k/ is spelled *c* more than *k*. /z/ is spelled *s* more than *z*. /j/ is spelled *g* more than *j*.
/th/	thumb	*th*
/ch/	chuck	*ch, tch, t*
/sh/	shout	*sh, sci, ch, s*
/ng/	lung	*ng, n*
/zh/	decision	*si*

(Inspired by *The Literacy Bug*; Hanna et al., 1966)

1 Explicitly and Systematically Teach Sound-Spelling Correspondences

Explicit, systematic instruction should continue long after children learn the alphabet. With that in mind, plan your phonics instruction using a clear scope and sequence, and teach sound-spelling correspondences directly—for example, "*c* and *h* together usually spell the sound /ch/. We can hear this sound at the beginning of words like *chat*. /ch/ is spelled *c-h*."

By being explicit and systematic in our instruction, we ensure that children do not have to rely on guessing or other less effective strategies to figure out words and word parts.

When we teach children two- and three-letter spelling patterns, such as *ee, oo, ai, sh*, and encourage them to use what they learn to decode words, their reading and spelling improve, even of unknown words (e.g., Christensen & Bowey, 2005; Savage & Stuart, 1998). One recent study by Vadasy and Sanders (2021) found that children can readily learn some two-letter spellings for phonemes even in kindergarten. By being explicit and systematic in our instruction, we ensure that children do not have to rely on guessing or other less effective strategies to figure out words and word parts.

On these two pages, you'll find a scope and sequence to help you cover common sound-spelling patterns after your students have learned the alphabet and before they begin multisyllabic-word reading.

SCOPE AND SEQUENCE FOR TEACHING COMMON SOUND-SPELLING CORRESPONDENCES	
Pattern	**Examples**
Sound-spelling patterns from the alphabet (i.e., regular VC words and CVC words)	Sample words: *at, it, is, am, can, bet, pin* Especially these word families: *-an, -ap, -at, -in, -ip, -it, -op, -ot, -ug*
Double-consonant endings	Sample words: *will, fizz, puss* Especially these word families: *-all, -ell, -ill -ss, -ff, -zz*
Common consonant digraphs	Sample words: *ship, chat, duck* *sh, th, ch, wh, ck* Especially these word families: *ack, ock, uck, ick*
Common consonant blends and digraphs	Sample words: *black, glass, pluck, skunk, dump* Beginning words: *bl-, br-, cl-, cr-, dr-, fr-, fl-, gl-, gr-, pl-, pr-, sl-, sm-, sp-, st-, tr-, tw-* Ending words: *-nk, -nt, -st, -mp, -ng*
Basic r-controlled vowel patterns	Sample words: *car, trip, burn* *-ar, -er, -ir, -or, -ur*
CVCe	Sample words: *brave, mute, rate* Focus on medial *a, i, o,* and *u* (CeCe is very rare in single-syllable words)

SCOPE AND SEQUENCE FOR TEACHING COMMON SOUND-SPELLING CORRESPONDENCES

Pattern	Examples
Vowel teams	Sample words: *play, coat, clue, book, tool, light* long *a* (*ai, ay*) long *e* (*ee, ea*) long *o* (*oa, ow*) long *u* (*ue, ew*) *oo* (both sounds) long *i* (*-y, igh*)
Diphthongs	Sample words: *coy, flaw, cow* *oi, oy* *aw, au* *ow, ou*
More spellings for *r*-controlled vowels	Sample words: *core, fear, lair, peer* *or* (sound)—multiple spellings: *or, ore, our* *er* (sound)—multiple spellings: *ir, er, ur, ear* *air* (sound)—multiple spellings: *are, air, ear* *ear* (sound)—multiple spellings: *ear, eer*
More common or highly useful consonant spelling patterns	Sample words: *stretch, dodge, enough* Such as: *ph-* *gh-* *-tch* *-dge* *thr-* *-ngth* *-eigh-* *-ough-*

(Based on Foorman et al., 2016)

2 Follow an Efficient and Effective Routine

Much like the alphabet, sound-spelling relationships can be taught and reinforced using efficient and effective routines that don't need to take a ton of time. Though you might need to do some isolated phonemic awareness work, it is critical, at this stage, to make letters part of that work, too. This is the best way to ensure children continue to develop control over the sounds in our language (e.g., NRP, 2000). Below is an example of a routine you can use to introduce a new sound-spelling relationship to the whole class or in small groups.

A POSSIBLE ROUTINE FOR INTRODUCING SOUND-SPELLING RELATIONSHIPS	
Phonemic Awareness Warm-Up	• Have children blend sounds to create words. Repeat 8 times. • Have children segment words to say sounds. Repeat 8 times. • Have children change one sound in a word to create a new word. Repeat 5 times. Have more time? You can put several routines together to create a longer lesson, such as doing a full phonemic awareness routine before this one.
Review	Review recently learned spellings.
Sound-Spelling Introduction	• Show the spelling. "This is one way to spell the sound ___. Say ___." "(spelling) spells (sound). Repeat after me." • Show the spelling in several words. If there are any relevant spelling rules, share with students. • If there are other ways to spell this sound that children already know, discuss them now.
Word Reading	Have children decode 8 to 10 words (at least half should have the target sound-spelling relationship), saying each sound and blending the sounds back together.
Spelling	Have children spell 8 to 10 words (at least half should have the target sound-spelling relationship), saying each sound to spell each part of the word.
Connection to Reading and Writing	• Remind children they should use these skills during real reading and writing. If children are about to engage in another activity where reading or writing is needed, make a direct connection to that activity. • Close by showing the spelling. Have children tell a partner what sound the spelling represents.

(Based on Fien et al., 2015)

You'll notice this routine includes both reading and spelling because, as I've pointed out, spelling supports reading—specifically, it improves phonics knowledge and word reading (Møller et al., 2021), and it is easy to integrate into your instruction. It is also important for later literacy outcomes (Treiman et al., 2019).

> **What About Spelling Tests?**
>
> Just say no to random word-list spelling tests! If you want to assess *encoding* (i.e., applying sound-spelling knowledge to spell words), give short informal assessments in which children spell new words that include the sound-spelling patterns you're teaching. For example, if you're teaching *ar*, ask children to spell *bar*, *par*, and *far* to check if they're able to apply that pattern to spelling words.

3 Respond to Children's Specific Sound-Spelling Needs in Whole Group and Small Groups

The best way to ensure systematic introduction of sound-spelling relationships to all the children in your classroom, especially in kindergarten and first grade, is by introducing them in whole-class instruction. All children can benefit from explicitly learning high-utility sound-spelling relationships.

But, as with all foundational skills instruction, phonics instruction is most impactful when you differentiate it (Puzio et al., 2020). Ensure you are responding to children's needs appropriately by monitoring their progress. Once you've identified each child's needs, follow up with differentiated small-group instruction. In addition to using your school or district's published assessments, continuously monitor children's learning of the sound-spelling relationships you are teaching by systematically observing and assessing them as they read and write.

Systematic observation requires making a plan to observe children. For example, once a week, you might take notes on children's word reading in a decodable text (see Chapter 8 for more on this) and their spelling during science, social studies, math, or writing. This will give you critical information about how well children are transferring their developing phonics skills.

Assessments do not necessarily have to be computerized, mandated, or lengthy. At the beginning of a small-group lesson, you could ask children to independently spell five words with target sound-spelling correspondences, collect their lists, and analyze the words for correct spellings and estimated spellings. Activities like this should not take the place of more formal assessments. However, they can help you understand the extent to which children are grasping and applying sound-spelling knowledge.

4 Support Sound-Spelling Knowledge With Other Foundational Skills and in Real Reading Contexts

As I discuss in greater detail in Chapter 8, the goal of sound-spelling instruction is to give children the tools they need to read and spell. Using sound-spelling knowledge in context, through decoding and encoding, makes that knowledge useful and creates readers.

ESSENTIAL INSTRUCTIONAL SWAP

Fewer Random Phonics Activities, More Reading and Spelling Opportunities

The whole point of phonics instruction is to teach word reading and spelling, so children should be reading and spelling words a lot. Focus on your purpose. Why teach sound-spelling correspondences and related spelling rules? To give children the necessary knowledge to decode new words and spell each sound in a developmentally appropriate way. Though there are many fun phonics activities out there, the most efficient and effective ones include tons of reading and spelling. Your activities should also include as many practice opportunities for each child as possible (e.g., Fien et al., 2015). Therefore, children should do lots of hands-on work, such as writing and using manipulatives (such as letter titles), whether you're teaching the whole class, small groups, or individuals, or students are working individually or in pairs, to apply as much cognitive effort as possible.

Effective and Efficient Routines for Sound-Spelling Instruction

Below are two routines that reinforce sound-spelling relationships by focusing on reading, reading, reading, and spelling, spelling, spelling!

	ROUTINES FOR SOLIDIFYING SOUND-SPELLING CORRESPONDENCES
Word Making/ Building	1. Give children a set of letter tiles (*a, r, t, g, u*). 2. Review the sound-spelling correspondences of the tiles. 3. Model using the tiles to make a word, such as *rat*. 4. Use prompts such as, "Make the word *rug*. Now change it to the word *tug*. Change the middle sound to /a/ (short *a*). What word did you make?" 5. Record the words children make on cards or the whiteboard. 6. As a group, sort the words based on sound-spelling correspondences, such as medial short *u* versus medial short *a*. Notice the spelling connections to these sounds. Have children come up with additional words that fit in those categories. (inspired by Cunningham & Cunningham, 1992)
Word Ladders	Students grow as readers and writers with these fun, engaging, reproducible word-building activities from Timothy V. Rasinski (see his Daily Word Ladder series). They read clues on each rung, and then change and rearrange letters to create words until they reach the top of the ladder. All the while, they're analyzing sound-symbol relationships, broadening their vocabulary, and building spelling skills. 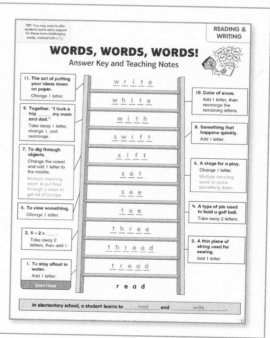

You can also adjust popular activities to include more reading and spelling, such as word sorts and picture sorts, which, when carried out the traditional way, can go wrong very easily. Imagine this: A child has 15 word cards in front of her that she is sorting for medial vowels. She can sort all those words successfully without decoding a single word by simply looking at the form of the medial vowel and, therefore, gaining no knowledge of sound-spelling correspondences. In other words, she can see the target letter without connecting any letters to sounds.

But, with a few quick fixes, word sorts and other kinds of decontextualized activities can be made more powerful by making sure:

- The activity is oral, *not* silent. Children need to be talking to hear themselves decoding words. If they're silent, they aren't decoding.

- Every child is participating by decoding and encoding words in isolation. Use strategies such as decoding in turn-and-talks and encoding on individual whiteboards to increase participation in large groups.

- Every child has *lots* of practice opportunities. One study found that children whose phonics lessons included 1.8 independent practice opportunities per minute had better outcomes than other children (Fien et al., 2015).

- Again, think about your goal for this activity. Are you hoping children will hear certain phonemes? See certain spellings? If your goal is for children to connect sounds to spellings, then add another layer: spelling! Pair your students, and have one child read a word as the other child spells it on a sheet of paper. Then ask the two children to sort the words together.

As a rule of thumb, whenever you assign decontextualized sound-spelling activities, expect your classroom to be loud. Encourage children to say, read, sound out, blend, and segment as much as they need to. Always encourage them to try to decode words during the activity.

Do It Tomorrow!

Make a quick shift in your phonics lesson tomorrow by adjusting a routine you already know and love. Take inspiration from my suggestions here about word sorts. See if you can add more word reading, spelling, and noise (yes, noise) into your phonics lesson tomorrow to make sure children are not only learning sound-spelling correspondences, but applying them, too.

Consider activities that not only build your students' knowledge of sound-spelling correspondences, but also deepen their knowledge of spelling rules. For example, you might have them sort words with the /oy/ sound spelled *oi* and *oy*, and words without the /oy/ sound. By doing that, they will not only learn that the /oy/ sound can be spelled two different ways, but also that *oi* usually comes in the middle of words (e.g., *boil*), whereas *oy* usually comes at the end (e.g., *boy*).

Bringing It Together

Sound-spelling correspondences are the meat of phonics instruction. In the early years, we should aim to teach the highest utility sound-spelling correspondences, from the alphabet to the most common single-syllable CVC words, to more sophisticated common patterns, covering all 44 phonemes. That will allow children to access more complex patterns and give them a base to learn new words as they encounter them in reading.

At the end of the day, however, sound-spelling knowledge is essentially just a bunch of facts. You might win *Jeopardy* with isolated sound-spelling knowledge, but if you want to win at reading and writing instruction, your students must be able to apply that knowledge. Our focus of phonics instruction should always be on reading and spelling. When children realize they can use sound-spelling knowledge to read and spell words, it is a proud moment for the teacher. My undergraduate methods students felt that pride, when, for example, one of them supported a child in adding a final *-s* to a word. Small moves like that led to many more throughout the semester, with children becoming better users of phonics to read and write.

As a rule of thumb, whenever you assign decontextualized sound-spelling activities, expect your classroom to be loud. Encourage children to say, read, sound out, blend, and segment as much as they need to.

In the next chapters, I'll dive even further into the interconnections among all the foundational skills and how, when connected appropriately, they lead to decoding, fluency, and reading comprehension.

CHAPTER 8

USING THE ELEMENTS TO DECODE WORDS

Foundational skills alone do not a word reader make. Each "element" described in Chapters 3 to 7 gives children a component skill to decode words. But teaching those skills in isolation is not enough. We must also give children opportunities to integrate those skills to become proficient decoders. Decoders use all the foundational skills to recognize new words (primarily by blending sounds and spellings). They can apply these sets of knowledge to read words by themselves and words in books. Children who are learning to decode strategically are on their way to proficient, fluent reading.

Consider children encountering a new text with unfamiliar words. They must have the set of knowledge and skills outlined in the chart below.

In this chapter, I show you how to move students from having foundational skills to being decoders. We know from Chapter 2 that being a decoder is a critical step in becoming a proficient reader. Because I've already focused on the importance of decoding, this chapter focuses on principles and swaps to ensure children learn how to decode, using the foundational skills described thus far.

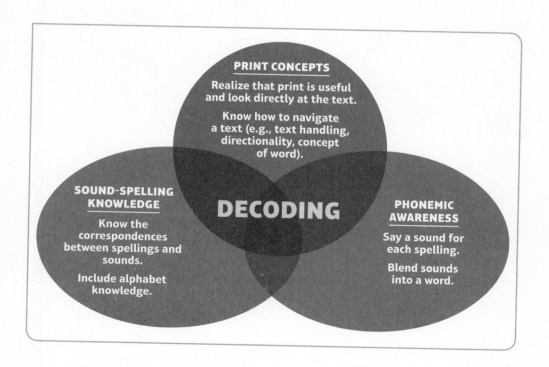

Principles of Great Decoding Instruction

Taking what we know from research and practice, here are four principles of great decoding instruction.

1 Explicitly and Systematically Address Decoding

What does it mean to teach decoding? You may find it strange to separate decoding from sound-spelling knowledge. I am not suggesting that these skills should be decoupled. Indeed, the Essential Instructional Swap in Chapter 7 is all about understanding sound-spelling relationships while decoding and encoding. I'm elevating decoding, calling it out from typical phonics, for three reasons.

Three Reasons I Call Out Decoding From Phonics

1. **We do not tend to give decoding the prominence it deserves.** In many phonics curricula, decoding is seen as the product of other instruction, the automatic result of knowing how letters and sounds relate to make words. Of course, many of us know that is not true. Most of us have worked with students who can score 100 percent on any phonics test and say each sound in a word, but simply cannot seem to blend the sounds of that word. Well then, add in oral phonemic awareness practice. Problem solved! In Chapter 5, I emphasized that, according to research, phonemic awareness is most productive when paired with letters. Phonemic blending plus sound-spelling is, indeed, decoding. Decoding is embedded in the instructional swaps throughout this book because it is the key to using all skills to read.

2. **Decoding can be and should be taught, modeled, and practiced.** Instead of making children leap from print concepts, phonemic awareness, and sound-spelling knowledge to decoding without support, model how you decode a word using the sound-spelling correspondence they've most recently learned. For example, show them the word *truck*, say, "This is how you read a word," and model how to pronounce each sound. Talk aloud about the various skills you are using (e.g., "I know I can say each sound that is spelled in this word. I know I can blend sounds together."). Decoding shouldn't be a secret or a by-product of print concepts, phonemic awareness, and sound-spelling knowledge. It should be purposefully taught so that children know exactly what to do when they encounter a new word.

3. **Decoding is utterly critical to success in reading.** In Chapter 2, I explained why decoding is hot and deserves to be. It is the best strategy for readers in the moment, *and* it is the best way to ensure long-term memory of words.

You should explicitly and systematically teach decoding, along with print concepts, phonemic awareness, and sound-spelling knowledge. See principles of instruction on the next page.

PRINCIPLES OF DECODING INSTRUCTION

Sound-Spelling	Print Concepts	Phonemic Awareness	Decoding
Early alphabet instruction	Most print concepts should be taught along with your alphabet instruction.	Isolating phonemes	Model blending to decode/read words during read-alouds and shared reading. Model segmenting to encode/spell words during writing. Explicitly call out that you are using phonemic awareness and phonics knowledge to do these tasks.
Middle alphabet instruction		Blending and segmenting orally	Have children decode and encode two-letter and three-letter words that begin with continuous sounds. Use Elkonin boxes with letters to support this work.
Continual review of basic letter-sound correspondences		Blending and segmenting orally	Have children decode and encode three-letter, three-sound words (CVC words).
Consonant digraphs		Some limited blending, segmenting, and manipulating orally	Have children decode and encode four-letter, three-sound words (words with common consonant digraphs).

2 Use Efficient and Effective Routines

Just like all foundational skills, decoding instruction shouldn't take all day. Decoding practice, however, should take all day, meaning children should be applying their skills in all the reading they do throughout the day. All three instructional swaps on pages 114 to 125 focus on real reading experiences. Just like the swaps in other chapters, they are research-based and do not take hours a day. Decoding practice can happen any time children see words, which sends a message that decoding is a powerful tool, and not just a thing to do during phonics.

3 Respond to Children's Specific Needs Based on Assessment

Differentiated instruction is key for reading achievement (Puzio et al., 2020). To differentiate, you first need to know each of your students' needs. If you teach kindergarten or first grade, most of your students are likely to need instruction in decoding, and the best way to find out for sure is through ongoing assessment, such as:

- A phonemic awareness assessment, such as the one described in Chapter 4. Children should be able to isolate and generate phonemes. They should also be able to blend and segment two- and three-sound words orally with some help from you.

- An alphabet knowledge assessment, such as in Chapter 5. Children should demonstrate mastery of most of the alphabet before you dive into decoding instruction. Those who are missing some letters can begin decoding if you devote time to helping them learn those letters.

Four Assessments to Determine Progress in Decoding

When children are learning to decode words, there are four major ways to assess their progress, depending on what you are trying to learn about a child. You should aim to assess children's learning fairly frequently, as much as once a week for children with many needs.

1. **Word decoding and spelling in isolation** For a quick informal check of a child's ability to apply sound-spelling correspondences to individual words, ask him or her to read or spell words with sound-spelling correspondences you've recently taught. You can integrate findings into your instruction by collecting or observing some children's spelling. This is an excellent option to ensure children are on track with your phonics lessons.

   If children cannot decode or spell words with the sound-spelling relationships you've been teaching, try words with a previously taught sound-spelling correspondence to identify if this challenge is ongoing or specific to one skill. Organize a small group or individual lesson to address this gap in student knowledge.

2. **Word reading and writing during other tasks** Another way to quickly and informally check children's decoding and spelling is to monitor them during tasks unrelated to phonics instruction. For example, collect or observe student writing during science. When they come to a word that includes taught sound-spelling correspondence, do they use this knowledge to spell?

   If a child cannot decode or spell words while engaged in other tasks, but can decode and spell words in isolation, organize a small group, individual lesson, or even whole-group modeling of transferring phonics knowledge into other tasks. In particular, check your language around reading words and spelling throughout the day. Use consistent language from your phonics instruction so children are better able to transfer that knowledge.

3. **Decoding inventory** A decoding inventory is another excellent way to monitor children's decoding abilities in context. I recommend Duke and colleagues' Listening to Reading protocol (2020). (You can find this on Nell Duke's website, nellkduke.org.) You can also fairly easily make your own decoding inventory to focus on decoding, like the one on the next page. Decoding inventories are a lot like a running record but with a few important differences. First, you can do a decoding inventory with any book. Second, you can observe and note errors without thinking about cuing. Third, though you can ask comprehension questions if you so choose, there are not prescribed questions to ask. There is not necessarily a formal set of comprehension questions for decoding inventories. Try giving a decoding inventory with a decodable text to see if children's decoding abilities are transferring to reading.

You can use any book for a decoding inventory, though I recommend a decodable book, such as those at my website, Beyond Decodables (beyonddecodables.com). Choose a book or a selection from a book and make note of how a student is decoding target words on the page.

Decoding Inventory

Instructions: Ask the child to read the text aloud. In the column on the right, note misreads he or she makes while reading. Record how the child attempts to read words (for example, *says each sound* or *looks to me for help when stuck*). Focus on words with sound-spelling relationships you've recently taught.

Extension: After reading, ask a few basic questions to ensure the child understood the text. Use the child's answers to help inform next steps in decoding.

Name: Dasani	Date: 1/21

Title of Text: *Kick It!* (selection) by Julia Lindsey	

Focus Decoding Skill: CVC-s and -ck	

Text:	Notes about child's misreads
Nick runs on the grass.	Runs = run (pause) s; did not blend back together
Nick gets the ball.	
He zigs. He zags.	Zags = zag (long pause) zag (pause) s
Nick kicks.	
The ball is in the net!	Net = said goal

Notes about the child's reading and patterns in misreads:

- Dasani was inconsistent in blending the final -s sound with CVC words and words with *-ck*.
- She consistently read *-ck* correctly.
- She sometimes wasn't looking at the words on the page and instead was reading what words she anticipated instead.

Decoding next steps:

- Practice blending final -s sound with CVC words
- Prompt Dasani to read the words off the page instead of anticipating words by reminding her: "Look at the word." "Use everything you know about letters and sounds to figure out that word." "Slide through all the sounds."

4. **District or school-based assessments** These more formal reading assessments can sometimes give you a lot of information about your readers and sometimes very little. The best way to use the reports you receive from district- and school-based assessments, especially computerized ones, is comparing this data to the data you've collected using the above three informal modes of assessment. Look for inconsistencies in student performance, which might be a red flag that you are missing a child's needs, or you need to help the child navigate the computerized assessment. Once you've gathered data about children's needs in decoding and spelling, you can form small groups based on needs.

4 Support Foundational Skills With Other Foundational Skills and in Real Reading Contexts

In addition to explicitly teaching correspondences between sounds and spellings, you need to offer explicit instruction, modeling, and supported practice in decoding words. Children need both decontextualized (words and sounds in isolation) practice and contextualized (words and sounds in real texts) practice. We know from research that the most effective approaches to teaching foundational reading, ranging from studies on Direct Instruction approach (Stockard et al., 2018; Ryder et al., 2006) to observations of exceptional teachers (Taylor et al., 2000) to studies of effective interventions (Fien et al., 2015), include lots of moments of decontextualized practice with words.

However, just as we now know that incidental phonics instruction in context isn't enough for most children to become readers (NRP, 2000), we also know that decontextualized practice alone isn't enough, either. If we want children who can apply phonics in context (which, again, is the whole point of phonics), then we need to also give them contextualized opportunities to apply phonics to decode and encode words within real texts.

What About Sight Words?

The term "sight word" is misleading. Sight words are words that readers can recognize on sight because they've stored them in long-term memory (Ehri, 2020). If you just read the last sentence without needing to pause and think, then all the sentence's words are sight words to you. Just as it would be inefficient to memorize every single word in the last sentence and the ones before it, it is inefficient to ask children to memorize "sight words." Instead, have children learn to read words that appear frequently in texts (i.e., high-frequency words) exactly as they learn to read any other word: by uncovering the connections between the letters in a word and the sounds they represent; in other words, by learning how to create orthographic maps of the words.

There's no reason to believe that children need to learn high-frequency words by rote memorization for several reasons. Most high-frequency words *are* regular words. They just might include sound-spelling correspondences children haven't learned yet. For example, the word *now* is a regular word with *n* representing its typical sound /n/ and *ow* representing the diphthong /ow/. If you need to teach this word before children learn diphthongs, it might seem irregular, and therefore you may think children should just memorize it. However, children are better able to remember words when they know the connections of the letters and sounds. We can instead help children explore the relationship between sounds and spellings of high-frequency words, because those words are not nearly as extraordinary as we may think they are.

To focus on orthography to teach high-frequency words, evaluate how and when you typically teach those words. After your initial instruction, give children opportunities to encounter those words in isolation and in books, and to spell them. When they do encounter those words, encourage them to decode them if necessary, using sound-spelling knowledge. To teach the word *now*, for example, you might say:

> This is the word now. In this word, we can hear that the letter n represents the sound /n/ and the letters o-w do something a little interesting. They come together to make the sound /ow/. Say the sound /ow/ with me. The word now is spelled n-o-w. Can you think of any words that sound like now at the end? What about the word how? What sounds do you hear in the word how? Using what we just learned about now, do your best to represent the sounds in how with letters on your whiteboard. In the words how and now, the sound /ow/ is represented with the spelling ow.

ESSENTIAL INSTRUCTIONAL SWAP 1

More Decodable Texts, Fewer Non-Decodable Texts

It's time to stop being doubtful of decodable texts! If our goal is efficient and effective foundational skills instruction and practice, we must give children what they need, if we're to meet that goal. If children are learning to decode words, we must give them texts with lots of words they can decode. Decodable texts are best used for developing decoders, likely in kindergarten through some of second grade, to bolster children's decoding in context.

It's time to stop being doubtful of decodable texts! If our goal is efficient and effective foundational skills instruction and practice, we must give children what they need, if we're to meet that goal.

Imagine you are a first-grade teacher, and your student knows the common sounds of individual letters and consonant digraphs. She is working on decoding regular words with common consonant digraphs, such as *chip* and *rush*. Which text on the next page will give her the chance to practice that skill?

Rick sits on the dock. He can see trash on the dock.

Text A

Sam told a scary story.

"Boo!" Sam yelled.

Everyone was afraid.

"I will turn on the light so that we can be calm," said Sam.

Text B

It's quite clear that Text A will give your student the chance to practice decoding words that include sound-spelling correspondences she knows, while Text B would require an entirely different set of knowledge and skills.

Text A is from a set of decodable texts for most children at the beginning of first grade. To read the text, a child needs to know:

- How to blend up to four sounds to read a word
- The common sounds letters represent (e.g., *r* represents /r/)
- The short vowel sounds and spellings (e.g., *i* represents short /i/)
- The sounds represented by common consonant digraphs (e.g., *ck* represents /k/)
- Some high-frequency words that are beyond the reader's current phonics knowledge (e.g., *do*, *see*, *they*)
- The meaning and sound of the ending *-s* (e.g., plural, /s/)

The word *trash* might challenge children who haven't learned to read consonant blends. However, because the first two letters represent their most common sounds, they may be able to read the consonant blend, *tr*, without much support. Ideally, a child entering first grade should have experienced phonics lessons that cover all the above-mentioned "need-to-knows." If that's not the case, you can support him or her with prompts such as, "Say each sound in the word" and "Remember, *c-k* spells /k/. Try to read the word with that in mind."

Text B is a mock Fountas and Pinnell Level E text that I wrote, also designed for the beginning of first grade. In this text, a child needs to know:

- How to blend up to five sounds to read a word
- How to chunk letters or spellings to read multisyllabic words
- The common sounds letters represent
- The short-vowel sounds and spellings, long-vowel sounds and spellings (e.g., *ai* in *afraid*)
- High-frequency words that are beyond the reader's current phonics knowledge (e.g., *everyone*, *was*)

Though this text includes some words a reader will likely be able to decode (*Sam*, *will*) and high-frequency words (*was*, *that*), many of the remaining words (*afraid*, *everyone*, *calm*, *scary*) will probably be extremely difficult for the child to decode. Instead, he or she would need to rely on guessing, context clues, teacher prompts, and random prior knowledge—strategies that are not as efficient or effective as decoding, and don't necessarily promote independence. If a child needs to rely on you or a picture to read nearly half the words on the page, the text and skills learned in the text are not supporting a child's independence as a reader.

Text A, unsurprisingly, is a decodable text. Decodable texts contain a high number of words with sound-spelling correspondences that a child has already learned. Theoretically, those texts complement our sound-spelling instruction because they let children use skills they've acquired in context.

Research supports the value of reading decodable texts:

- Readers are likely to be more accurate, rely less on the teacher, and apply phonics more frequently (Mesmer, 2005).

- Early exposure to decodable texts may help children rely more on decoding and less on guessing over time (Juel & Roper-Schneider, 1985).

- Decodable texts support all young readers and are more likely to support beginning decoders at any grade level and multilingual learners better than other books can (see synthesis by Cheatham & Allor, 2012; Chu & Chen, 2014).

Well-written decodable texts increase independence and proficiency (because readers can decode the words), as well as motivation (because well-written decodable texts aren't meaningless).

Is this a home run for decodable texts? Well, no. There is no research (yet) that says children should read decodable texts exclusively, nor is there research that says decodable text reading is better than reading other kinds of books.

What is a home run for decodable texts? They fit our purpose here—they allow children to practice decoding in a real context efficiently and effectively. Well-written ones increase independence and proficiency (because readers can decode the words), and as well as motivation (because well-written decodable texts aren't meaningless). See page 121 for my criteria for selecting good decodable texts.

An Effective and Efficient Routine for Using Decodable Texts

Below is one routine for how to use decodable texts. It shouldn't feel too different from other types of small-group reading instruction. The major change is the emphasis on decoding; before, during, and after reading.

AN EXAMPLE OF A SMALL-GROUP LESSON WITH A DECODABLE TEXT	
Introduce the text	Introduce the text with a one-sentence connection to prior knowledge or a reason for reading beyond "because it's time to read."
Prepare children for reading	• Explicitly teach or review the appropriate phonics knowledge or decoding strategy. • Model and help children practice reading and writing words in isolation, using the knowledge or strategy. • Review high-frequency words by having children read or write the word.
Ask children to read the text	Remind children to say each sound in the word and slide through the sounds. **Ways to support different types of readers:** • For children who may benefit from support: Use echo reading: read each line/page and then have children repeat after you while tracking the print. • For children who may be ready to read independently: Read the first page together. Watch to ensure children are tracking print. Encourage children to whisper-read independently. Listen in on children's reading and prompt as needed. • For children who are reading independently: Point out and model reading a few of the not-yet-decodable words to support more fluent reading. Encourage children to whisper-read independently. **Prompts for different types of words:** • Decodable words (Duke, 2020): "Look at the word." "Say each sound." "Slide through the sounds." • For words with many features beyond a child's abilities: "That word is _____." • For high-frequency words: "Remember, in this word the spelling _____ represents the sound _____."
Ask questions	Ask a series of questions to check children's comprehension. Relate the questions to the original purpose for reading, when appropriate.
Send off	Have children demonstrate to the group or a partner how they used decoding to read a word in the text. Remind children how they can use their knowledge of phonics whenever they read.

Finding Decodable Texts

The best decodable texts aren't just decodable. They also:

- Contain high-frequency words
- Repeat words (recall that readers normally need to decode a word a few times to orthographically map it)
- Are meaningful—they tell a good story or offer fascinating facts
- Are culturally appropriate and responsive
- Contain natural language and syntax
- Contain vocabulary that is familiar to young children

When searching for decodable texts, makes sure the publishers of those texts are transparent about what's in them. They should include a scope and sequence for the phonics elements in each text, as well as clearly stating if they considered other factors, such as the ones above. If you need a place to start, try these resources:

- **Beyond Decodables (beyonddecodables.com)**
  My website contains over 60 texts written with or by educators in the Boston Public Schools that are (among other things) decodable, meaningful, and culturally responsive.

- **Text Project (textproject.org)**
  Dr. Freddy Hiebert's website contains many texts written to be (among other things) decodable. The books include lots of high-frequency words and repetition.

- **Phonics First Little Readers (shop.scholastic.com/teachers)**
  This is a full library of enjoyable, easy-to-manage decodable readers. The durable box houses 120 books (5 copies of 24 titles) and a teaching guide filled with lessons and tips for helping children decode words.

Leaning Into Big Worries

This swap is a big one because it will likely mean using a new or different type of text in instruction. So, I recommend starting slowly by swapping one small-group reading lesson a week for a decodable-text lesson. Challenge yourself to change your instruction to match the purpose of using decodable texts: to improve your students' word recognition. In other words, do not simply substitute in a decodable text for a leveled text in a guided reading lesson.

During the lesson, you might notice that your students' fluency *decreases*, and that is okay. In fact, it should be expected. When you transition children from using knowledge about words they already have to using new knowledge about phonics to decode words, reading may initially be more difficult for some of them. This is part of the process. Eventually, their fluency will improve and, as a huge bonus, they will develop orthographic maps, habits, and skills of advanced readers who can read complex words.

To boost the effectiveness of this swap, give children decodable texts at other points in the school day or at home. Remember, these texts encourage independence because they include words that a child can figure out with phonics knowledge. They can even reread the same text several times to build fluency. As you become more confident using decodable texts, you can introduce more small groups to them, targeting instruction to students' needs.

Quality Books Matter!

Resist the urge to use just "any old decodable." Aim for texts that are interesting and engaging, as well as culturally responsive. Matching texts to students' knowledge and interests may help them persist in challenging tasks (Fulmer & Frijters, 2011), such as learning to decode new words. Furthermore, children often find stories and texts that affirm their cultural identities and backgrounds more interesting (Cartledge et al., 2016; Piper, 2019). By giving them decodable texts that match their interests and backgrounds, we might increase motivation and joy in reading, while helping children navigate the complex task of decoding!

In one classroom where the teacher was using a series of decodable texts that I wrote, students practically swarmed me when they realized I was the author. "Tell us what happens next," they begged. Instead, I sat and listened to them read aloud books in the series they hadn't yet read. Joy can and should be central to your decodable instruction and is especially easy when you pick high-quality decodable texts.

What About My Current Classroom Library?

Please do not eliminate texts from your classroom library that aren't labeled "decodable." However, you might want to reorganize your library! Here are some ideas:

- Check for texts that you didn't realize are decodable. Some texts that fit into other categories (such as texts with alphabetic or numeric levels) may be decodable with certain phonics scope and sequences. You'll probably have to read those texts to confirm it. Save the texts that are decodable!

- Save texts for children who will likely not need to read decodable texts all year (especially if you teach first or second grade).

- Save trade books and books related to your content units. If children cannot read these texts themselves, use them for shared reading, partner reading, or read-alouds to support content learning.

- Resist the urge to create baskets for books that contain certain types of words: "Books with CVC words," "Books with Digraphs," for example.

  Instead, organize your library by genre and/or topic. When teaching children to select texts, you can encourage children to first select a genre or topic they are interested in and then try out a page. If they can't read the individual words, encourage them to try a different text on the same topic. By leading with interest and motivation, you're encouraging a strategy adult readers use to pick books (When was the last time you selected a book just because it was "just right" for your abilities?).

  Additionally, it is not the end of the world if a child picks a book he or she cannot read just yet— we can support reading time in different ways than just with the text.

Less Decoding for Phonics Instruction, More Decoding for Everyday Reading

Decoding isn't just for phonics tests. It's not even just for book reading. Decoding lets readers recognize words in any context. While some children easily make this generalization, many do not. One reason they might not realize they can use decoding to recognize any word is because they do not see it modeled, nor do they encounter decodable words throughout the day.

This instructional swap is directly from practice. An innovative coach in North Carolina, Elaine Shobert, and her teachers moved to focus more on decoding in the past few years. They integrated phonemic awareness into phonics lessons, started using some decodable texts, and changed their reading assessments in the early grades to identify skill-based needs. Walking the halls of Rock Rest Elementary, I could clearly see evidence of this focus. And, even more importantly, I could see clear evidence for how much these children loved reading and loved being able to independently decode words.

Elaine wanted to build on this success. She noticed children were still not leveraging their newfound decoding skills at other times of day. In particular, she noticed that some children who were struggling to decode in context were the same ones who struggled to understand word problems in math. Noticing these were likely connected challenges, Elaine created a series of decodable math word problems, targeting children's word recognition and their math problem-solving skills in one moment.

This is a great example of an efficient, effective practice connected to real reading, and it works for other content areas. For example, you could make a map with decodable labels for a social studies or geography lesson. You could write a science investigation using decodable words, giving children the chance to read the instructions for the investigation. The sky is the limit.

Decodable Math Problems

To try out Elaine's decoding and math activity, you will need to write some decodable sentences—sentences for any purpose, from decodable texts, to decodable math problems, to decodable class instructions.

First, think about the phonics scope and sequence. Brainstorm a list of words that children can read and words that include recently taught sound-spelling correspondences. For example, if children can decode 3-grapheme, 3-sound words and they just learned *c-h* spells /ch/, you might have a list like *chip, chop, chin,* and *chat*. Second, think about your math scope and sequence. For example, you might be teaching addition word problems. Third, use your list in combination with your math content. Your train of thought might be something like this: *No one really adds together* chop *or* chin *or* chat, *but you can add* chips! *Children can also read number words like* six *and* ten, *which add to under 20, fitting our current math goal*. Next, draft a word problem using words children have learned to read. Be sure to include high-frequency words. Here's an example.

> Ben has six chips. Yum!
>
> His mom has ten chips.
>
> His mom says, "Ben, I am full. You can have my chips."
>
> Ben gets his mom's ten chips.
>
> How many chips does Ben have now?

Then, go through each word. Say it aloud and check to make sure it is decodable. In this case, decodable words are CVC words, words with *ch*, and high-frequency words.

DETERMINING DECODABILITY

1. All the words that you've explicitly taught are considered "decodable." For example, after you've taught the alphabet and blending/segmenting three-sound words, all regular consonant-vowel-consonant words are decodable.

2. All high-frequency words you've taught are decodable.

Count all the words that are not decodable. Count all the words in the book (this number is often printed somewhere in the book).

Decodability = [(total words—not decodable words)/total words] x 100

Decodable texts should be about 80 percent decodable.

Bold words are NOT decodable

Ben has six chips. Yum!
His mom has ten chips.
His mom says, "Ben, I am full. You can have my chips."
Ben gets his mom's ten chips.
How many chips **does** Ben **have now?**

85.71 percent = [(35-5)/35] x 100

My problem is 86 percent decodable.

Finally, revise your problem to make it more decodable or decide which parts you expect children to read. In my case, I would simply read the last sentence/question to students so that my word problem is 100 percent decodable.

To use your word problem in instruction, you will need to play a dual role of math teacher and reading teacher. This is likely easiest in small group. Approach the problem like a typical word problem. Then, call children's attention to the first word or sentence, prompting them to slide through the sounds to read. Prompt children as they read the word problem the same way you would if they were reading a decodable text. Celebrate children's ability to use phonics knowledge to read words, even during math! Encourage children to reread the problem as needed. Ask comprehension questions at the end or have children visualize the problem to help them understand the text and answer the math problem. Proceed with your typical math instruction to support children in answering the question.

Less Unsupported Independent Reading, More Supported Independent Reading

Shocking but true: Research does not consistently find that additional silent independent reading time supports children's reading outcomes (research reviewed in both Erbeli & Rice, 2021; National Reading Panel, 2000). It is critical to think about what this research suggests about what we need to do to ensure children's in-school reading time supports their reading outcomes.

Research is not suggesting eliminating time for children to read. The research above refers to *silent* and *unsupported* reading, not all types of reading. It is not wrong to give children time to choose books and let them attempt to read them. We know that having choice and agency is motivating and engaging to young readers. In addition to this type of reading time, however, we have to make slightly different choices to support decoding. When the purpose of independent reading time is to support decoding, then we need to think about how to best use that time to make it work for us and our students. Below, you'll find some semi-independent and tech-enabled reading activities that are likely to support decoding development.

Supported Decoding Activities

Most independent reading occurs during stations or centers. Using time most effectively for decoding skills is incredibly challenging. Sometimes, it seems like there are no good options, especially for our youngest learners. In my experience and according to the research (e.g., Taylor et al., 2000), the most effective teachers first spend significant time setting up the routines. Don't be afraid to spend time at the beginning of the year and periodically throughout the year setting expectations and supporting children in these types of semi-independent activities. This will give you more time back in uninterrupted small group and ensure this time is used wisely. Some activity options include:

- **Partner reading of decodable text** This can be based on shared interests or known science or social studies topics. Partners can help each other decode unknown words.

- **Rereading decodable books introduced in small group** Children can practice decoding words they have some familiarity with (recall it typically takes several chances to decode a word to create an orthographic map) and practice fluency through rereading.

- **Partner decoding games** First, teach children how to play a game that fits their needs in small group. Then, invite partnerships of children to play games without your support. One excellent free resource for these types of activities is the Florida Center for Reading Research.

- **Computerized decoding games** It's okay to rely on technology sometimes, and many apps for children have come a long way. Play around on the app or program first to make sure it includes reading and spelling. Check to make sure it fits your philosophy of reading so that it does not undermine your teaching.

- **Listening to digital read-alouds** This may not support decoding as precisely as other activities; however, children can have lots of choices to explore their interests in books they listen to from online platforms or apps. Listening to books is an excellent way to encourage reading when children are not quite ready to be independent readers themselves.

> ***Do It Tomorrow!***
>
> Just dive right in! If you've never used a decodable text before, I encourage you to download one from the sites mentioned in this chapter. Pick a text that matches the sound-spelling knowledge of a small group of children in your room and see what happens.
>
> If you're not quite ready for that step, try swapping out some of your typical prompts during small-group reading for more decoding-focused prompts, such as "slide through each sound," and see if children are better able to access new words.

Bringing It Together

Decoding is the secret sauce. It's the culmination and application of all foundational skills. It unlocks word reading and spelling. It's a route to long-term success. By specifically focusing ourselves on using foundational skills instruction to create decoders, we can have more targeted, purposeful instruction. We can also have clear, articulated goals for readers that are just about specific texts. For example, you might choose a goal such as, "All my kindergartners will be able to decode regular CVC words and CVCe words."

Use decoding-focused goals as guideposts for your instruction and as a reminder about all the foundational skills that go into decoding.

CHAPTER 9

ADDING THE ELEMENTS OF CHUNKING

When children can recognize the value of print, map sounds to print, and decode one-syllable words, they've made a huge step forward in word recognition. But they are not at the finish line. Most of the new words upper-elementary students encounter while reading are longer, multisyllabic words (Kearns et al., 2016), which, of course, are more challenging to read than one-syllable words (Duncan & Seymour, 2003; Muncer & Knight, 2012; Yap & Balota, 2009). Even children who can easily apply sound-spelling knowledge to single-syllable words may have difficulty reading multisyllabic words (Toste et al., 2017). To provide the best foundation for success in *all* types of word reading, not just one-syllable word reading, it is critical to consider a few more foundational skills.

In this chapter, I will share what we currently know about teaching children to decode multisyllabic words, focusing on what they may need in kindergarten through second grade to be more prepared for those words in later elementary school. I call this extension of decoding *chunking*.

Chunking Defined

As I noted in Chapter 1, decoding means using sound-spelling knowledge to read new words. And as I noted in Chapters 2 to 8, children need many types of foundational skills and knowledge about how the English language works to read individual one-syllable words. To read individual multisyllabic words efficiently and effectively, they need new skills and knowledge.

Chunking isn't typically thought of as "hot," the way decoding is. You rarely see people Tweeting about it or read articles arguing for or against it. One popular chunking-style strategy is "Chunky Monkey," where children identify multisyllabic words by finding parts of the word they know, including word families. However, in this chapter, I advocate for children using their knowledge about syllables (i.e., a word part with one vowel sound) and morphology (i.e., identifying and manipulating the smallest units of meaning in language) to chunk words into parts and to then decode those parts. Chunking is an extension of decoding, requiring all the elements of decoding and more. Just as with one-syllable word decoding, children must know how spellings relate to sounds to read multisyllabic words.

Chunking is an extension of decoding, requiring all the elements of decoding and more.

Reading multisyllabic words is not as simple as blending large numbers of phonemes or learning more complex spellings. Children need more than just sound-spelling knowledge to confidently conquer multisyllabic words for several reasons.

Three Reasons Children Need Word-Chunking Skills

1. Children can be successful in one-syllable decoding, but not so in multisyllabic chunking. Imagine trying to read a word like *raspberry* or *stegosaurus* sound by sound. Though theoretically possible to get close to accurately decoding those words by blending individual spellings and sounds, a child's working memory would be stretched to or past its limit (Heggie & Wade-Woolley, 2017). Additionally, extensive phonics knowledge does not necessarily predict a reader's ability to read a multisyllabic word (Kearns, 2015).

2. Many multisyllabic words contain complex sound-spelling patterns, relating more to morphology or etymology (i.e., the study of word origins) than alphabet knowledge. Multisyllabic words are often created by complex combinations of syllables, affixes, and root words from Latin and Greek, making them challenging for readers to

segment and decode (Bhattacharya, 2020). Think of words like *beautiful* and *photosynthesis*. If children do not have the knowledge to use morphology to read big words like those, they are likely to either skip those words while reading or rely on context only to recognize them, and therefore dilute their comprehension of the text (Toste et al., 2017).

3. Teaching children specific sets of knowledge (morphology) and skills (chunking) can improve their word reading. For example, teaching them to use syllable knowledge to analyze and segment words can improve their word reading (Bhattacharya & Ehri 2004; Moats, 2004; Muller et al., 2020). Teaching them to recognize and segment words using morphemes, particularly affixes and root words, can improve it, too (Gellert et al., 2021; Goodwin & Ahn, 2010; Reed, 2008). Furthermore, combining syllable instruction and morphology instruction may be particularly beneficial in supporting the widest range of multisyllabic word reading (Austin et al., 2021; Gray et al., 2018). Theoretically, instruction in splitting words into decodable chunks (some of which may also be meaningful chunks) allows children to decode multisyllabic words more quickly and accurately.

Explicitly and systematically teaching children how to chunk words should be hot! Once they are proficient single-syllable decoders, they need to start developing knowledge to read the tens of thousands of multisyllabic words they'll encounter in texts over their lifetimes.

Explicitly and systematically teaching children how to chunk words should be hot! Once they are proficient single-syllable decoders, they need to start developing knowledge to read the tens of thousands of multisyllabic words they'll encounter in texts over their lifetimes. Next, I'll discuss critical elements of chunking for the early grades. Consider the discussion a primer on the topic, not a deep dive, to set up young children for success in later grades.

The Elements of Chunking

Chunking means dividing a word into parts that can be decoded. To do that efficiently, a reader needs to know where the helpful divisions are in multisyllabic words, using, ideally, syllabication (i.e., dividing the word by its syllables) and morphology (i.e., dividing the word by its smallest units of meaning). Then, a reader needs to know what to do with those chunks. The best way to decode the individual chunks is by using sound-spelling knowledge (as discussed in the previous chapters), knowledge of other words, and, again, morphology.

Look at the text on the first page of *The Adventures of Captain Underpants*, the first book in Dav Pilkey's enormously popular series, which is considered readable for children in second grade and above.

Meet George Beard and Harold Hutchins. George is the kid on the left with the tie and the flat-top. Harold is the one on the right with the T-shirt and the bad haircut. Remember that now.

That's 36 words. Six of them are names, which tend to be irregular and may need to be already known by or provided to many children. Of the remaining 30 words, 27 are decodable, one-syllable words or high-frequency words. Only three words are multisyllabic words (*T-shirt*, *haircut*, and *remember*)—plus one hyphenated word (*flat-top*) that can be easily decoded if children know what to do with hyphens (another advanced print concept). Let's think about how chunking would help a reader decode those words.

HOW CHUNKING HELPS A READER DECODE WORDS FROM *THE ADVENTURES OF CAPTAIN UNDERPANTS*

T-shirt	haircut	remember
If a child knows to chunk at a hyphen and knows a letter on its own can say its name (such as *T*), he can most likely chunk this word into *T* and *shirt* by using sound-spelling knowledge to decode *shirt*, and then blend it with *T* to identify *T-shirt*.	If a child knows that compound words can be read by chunking them into smaller words OR if she knows that we can split two-syllable words between two consonants (in this case, *r* and *c*) to create two decodable chunks (*hair* and *cut*), she can most likely use sound-spelling knowledge to decode *hair* and *cut*, and blend to identify *haircut*.	This one might be a bit trickier because it's a trisyllable word. If a child knows that *re* is a prefix pronounced /r/ /ee/, he can first chunk the word into *re* and *member*. Then, if he knows that he can split two-syllable words in between two consonants (in this case, *m* and *b*) to create two decodable chunks (*mem* and *ber*), he can chunk the word further. By blending the chunks together, he can identify *remember*.

Put simply, a child who can proficiently read one-syllable words and has some knowledge of chunking to read multisyllabic words has a good chance at successfully reading this page from *The Adventures of Captain Underpants* (and, quite likely, the whole book). When reading multisyllabic words, children can and should flexibly use orthography and morphology flexibly (as well as sound-spelling knowledge) to decode chunks.

This example illustrates that successful chunking requires these elements:

- Knowledge of syllables and how to split words into chunks based on them
- Knowledge of morphology and how to split words into chunks based on morphemes (e.g., affixes and root words)
- The ability to decode chunks
- Knowing when to apply that knowledge and use that skill

Guess What? *The Adventures of Captain Underpants* **Is a Decodable Text!**

As you likely noticed, *The Adventures of Captain Underpants* is a decodable text for a child who knows common sound-spelling relationships, how to decode single-syllable words, and a little bit about using syllables and morphemes to chunk words. You'll start to notice that, by second grade, many, many books become decodables for your students. At this stage, children can transfer all their decoding knowledge to reading real, authentic texts.

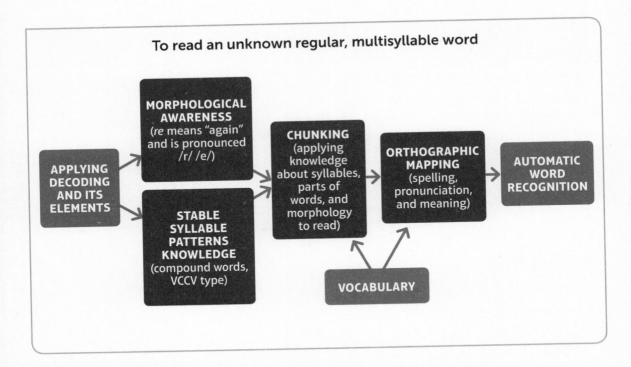

To read an unknown regular, multisyllable word

APPLYING DECODING AND ITS ELEMENTS

MORPHOLOGICAL AWARENESS (*re* means "again" and is pronounced /r/ /e/)

STABLE SYLLABLE PATTERNS KNOWLEDGE (compound words, VCCV type)

CHUNKING (applying knowledge about syllables, parts of words, and morphology to read)

ORTHOGRAPHIC MAPPING (spelling, pronunciation, and meaning)

AUTOMATIC WORD RECOGNITION

VOCABULARY

In the next sections, I dive into syllables and morphology. Then I show you wise ways to teach chunking that require students to use their knowledge of syllables and morphology, and their decoding skills.

Syllabication

Syllables are units of pronunciation. They contain one vowel sound that is preceded by or surrounded by a consonant or consonants (e.g., *water* = *wa* + *ter*). The easiest way to identify syllables is by noticing when your chin falls when you say a multisyllabic word. For example, when you say *water*, you most likely can feel and, if looking in a mirror, see your chin fall once upon saying *wa* and again upon saying *ter*.

Children tend to develop an awareness of syllables very early. Syllable awareness is part of phonological awareness and generally develops in preschool (Anthony & Francis, 2005; Juel & Minden-Cupp, 2000; Mesmer & Williams, 2015).

Why Syllables Matter for Word Reading

Research suggests that:

- Reading multisyllabic words requires a reader to process each syllable or unit (Kearns et al., 2016).

- Segmenting words into syllables can help readers recognize words (Bhattacharya, 2020; Bhattacharya & Ehri, 2004; Heggie & Wade-Woolley, 2017; Muller et al., 2020). When attempting to recognize a multisyllabic word, readers make decisions about pronunciations, using syllable units (Yap & Balota, 2009). They then decode each syllable unit based on their single-syllable, sound-spelling knowledge.

- Some syllabication programs, such as PHAST (Lovett et al., 2000), positively impact children's word reading because their creators took that research into consideration. In those programs, children are taught to analyze words using different types of syllables.

- Knowing about syllables may help children read new words by remembering words they've encountered in the past. In one study, Bhattacharya and Ehri (2004) taught children to analyze a word's syllables following these basic steps:

  1. Segment words into syllables and decode each unit.
  2. Match syllable pronunciations back to unit spellings.
  3. Blend units to try the word again.

Not only did children's decoding of words improve, but also their ability to spell those words later. This type of instruction enables children to analyze multisyllabic words, giving them a handy tool to use when they encounter them in reading.

Syllable work alone won't teach children how to read multisyllabic words. It is a start, though— and, as part of a larger effort to teach multisyllabic-word reading, it is powerful.

A word of warning, though: Teaching multisyllabic word reading exclusively through syllabication is a mistake. Syllable patterns may not be as rule-governed as we tend to believe. For example, one syllable rule says we should chunk a two-syllable word: 1) between the first vowel and the next consonant, and then 2) expect the first vowel to be the long sound. This works for words like *radar* (ra | dar) and *become* (be | come). But this "rule" only works about 30 percent of the time (Kearns, 2020).

This brings us to a challenge of teaching multisyllabic words: No one element is going to lead children to the correct pronunciation of every single multisyllabic word. As such, syllable work alone won't teach children how to read multisyllabic words. It is a start, though—and, as part of a larger effort to teach multisyllabic-word reading, it is powerful. In the next section, I will show you the most effective ways to help children chunk words using syllabication.

Principles of Great Syllable Instruction

Here are two general principles of syllable instruction in the early grades.

- **Build awareness that syllables exist and are useful.** Though most children should be able to hear syllables, check to be sure and give extra support as needed. You can do that by asking them what a syllable is, teaching them the "chin dropping" strategy described on the previous page, and giving them practice in listening for syllables.

- **Teach useful syllables, but don't overdo it.** In the early years, teach two types of multisyllabic words: two-syllable compound words, such as *birdcage*, and two-syllable VC|CV words, such as *number*, which contain very stable syllable patterns. To read compound words, encourage children to chunk based on the smaller words they see. That's a quick inroad into syllables! For example, children who can read CVC words with digraphs, and know how to chunk words into parts, are ready to learn to read words such as *dishpan* and *bathtub*.

To read two-syllable VC|CV words (which include many compound words), encourage children to divide syllables (chunk) at the two medial consonants.

Morphology

Here's some good news: You are probably already teaching some morphology, but you're not calling it that. Morphology is concerned with morphemes, the smallest units of meaning in words. If you teach children to add -ed to words to make them past tense and teach the three pronunciations of -ed (e.g., /id/ seated, /d/ lived, /t/ wished), you are teaching morphology. If you teach children to read compound words by breaking them into the two shorter words, you are teaching morphology.

Morphemes can be whole words. For example, you cannot break the word dog into smaller, meaningful pieces. Dog, all by itself, is a singular, meaningful unit. You might say, "But the word dog does contain the word do!" While that is true, the meaning and pronunciation of the word dog have nothing to do with the word do, and the letter g does not represent a meaningful unit. Thus, the word dog is one morpheme.

Compound Word Alert!

Compound words are not just multi-syllabic, they are multimorphemic. Teaching them blurs the line between teaching syllable division and teaching morphology. This blurring will come up again and again because most multimorphemic words have more than one syllable. It leads us straight to the essential instructional swap suggested on page 145: Chunking and reading multisyllabic words requires children to apply flexibly their knowledge of sound-spelling correspondences, decoding, syllables, morphology, and more.

Words can also have many morphemes. The word unhappiness has three morphemes. You can break unhappiness into the prefix un, which means "not," the root word happy, and the suffix ness, which indicates the state, quality, or condition of the root word. All three of those parts are meaningful all by themselves. That does not mean all morphemes can stand on their own—ness and un certainly can't. Morphemes that cannot stand on their own (un and ness) are called bound morphemes. Morphemes that can stand on their own as words (happy) are called free morphemes. Unlike do and g in dog, however, the meaning of un and ness contribute to the whole meaning of the word unhappiness.

BREAKING DOWN THE WORD *UNHAPPINESS*		
Morpheme	**Meaning**	**Word Part**
un	not	prefix
happy	joyful	root word
ness	the state of	suffix
unhappiness: not in a joyful state		

There are two other categories of morphemes: inflectional and derivational.

Inflectional Morphemes

Inflectional morphemes change a grammatical property of the word. By adding an inflectional morpheme to the end of a word, such as -*ed*, -*s*, or -*ing*, for example, you change the word's tense. By adding an inflectional morpheme to the end of a word, such as -*s*, you pluralize the word.

INFLECTIONAL MORPHEMES		
Goal	**Morphemes**	**Examples**
Change tense	-ed, -ing, -s, -es, -en	*Hopped* *Jumping* *Gallops* *Goes* *Eaten*
Change number	-s, -es	*Cats* *Boxes*
Indicate possession	's	*Mekhi's*
Compare	-er, -est	*Faster* *Strongest*

Derivational Morphemes

Derivational morphemes are affixes. Affixes are prefixes (which appear at the start of words) and suffixes (which appear at the end of words). They are added to root words to change the meaning and/or form of a word. Root words are the base words. In many cases, they can stand on their own or are slightly changed. *Happy* is the root word in the example above. Adding *dis-* to a word means "not" or the opposite of the word; *regard* and *disregard* are opposites. Adding *-ful* to a word means "full of" the word; *beautiful* means "full of beauty." There are many derivational morphemes. In the scope and sequence below, I define a few of them.

Unlike so many aspects of written English, affixes are incredibly stable in terms of meaning, spelling, and pronunciation. The affix *pre-* always means "before," it is always spelled p-r-e, and it is always pronounced /p/ /r/ /e/. The stability of affixes makes them helpful units for children to learn to spell and read.

Most morphology instruction focuses on derivational morphemes, which supports readers in three ways: 1) it allows them to use sound-spelling knowledge to decode each chunk (prefix, root, suffix); 2) it builds vocabulary; and 3) it facilitates spelling (O'Connor, 2015).

When analyzing a word's morphology, we usually ask children to look for roots and affixes. A challenge with that approach is that we, as adult readers, may not always know the meaning of the root word or affix. For example, you probably recognize that *reverse* has two morphemes: *re* and *verse*. But unless you've had a good reason to look it up, you probably don't know what *verse* in

A Word of Caution About Morphemes

A friend of mine, who is a longtime literacy coach, recently told me about a small group of children attempting to chunk the word *repeat* by grappling with the meaning of its root word *peat*…for over 45 minutes, losing valuable instructional time. The teacher was basing her instruction on *peat*, the organic material found in marshes that's often used by gardeners. But that meaning does not help us understand *repeat* at all. *Peat* was derived from the Latin word *petere*, which means to ask, seek, or pursue. This is not necessarily useful for reading and understanding *repeat* or other words; not to mention it complicates a relatively straightforward vocabulary word because most children already know the meaning of *repeat*. By contrast, taking the same prefix, *re*, we can consider words such as *redo* in a very different way. It is quite useful for children to grapple with the meaning of *re + do* by simply adding the affix's meaning to the root: do again. For words such as *repeat*, encourage children to use the morphemes as chunks to decode while separately learning the entire word's meaning, instead of putting too much emphasis on how the meaning is constructed.

reverse means. *Verse* is a Latin root word that means "to turn." *Re* is a prefix that means "back" or "again." Thus, *reverse* means "to turn again" or "to turn back."

It is important to know the meanings of word parts prior to your instruction. However, it is equally important to know when it may not be useful to discuss the meaning of a morpheme at length with a young child. Sometimes, at the early stage in a child's reading development, it is more efficient to focus on decoding a word's morpheme(s) and not necessarily the meaning of its morpheme(s).

Principles of Great Morphology Instruction

For truly effective morphology instruction, specifically in the early grades, keep in mind these two principles:

- **Focus on utility.** Though studies with older children show the power of deep morphological analysis to infer word meanings, combining decoding instruction with vocabulary instruction (e.g., Austin et al., 2021), it's not as clear that this is the best instructional strategy in early grades (e.g., Michaud et al., 2017). Instead, when you first introduce morphemes for word recognition, I suggest starting with utility for decoding and using words children already know. For example, you can break apart words like *playing* (*play / ing*) and *helper* (*help / er*) to decode them and have some discussions about how these parts inform the meaning without needing to construct the meaning of an unknown word.

- **Follow a reasonable scope and sequence to teach morphology explicitly.** In the scope and sequence below, you'll notice that I focus on affixes that are:

    1. likely to be easily understood by young children.
    2. relatively high frequency.
    3. typically decodable with regular sound-spelling knowledge.

Recall that the purpose of chunking is to segment a word into parts that can be decoded. Starting with affixes that children are likely to be able to decode, and therefore eliminating the need to teach new sound-spelling patterns, can help children access two-syllable words. This is not an exhaustive scope or sequence, but rather a starting point.

MORPHOLOGY INSTRUCTION SEQUENCING		
Morpheme	**Teaching Move**	**Examples**
Inflectional morphemes -s, -es, -ing, -ed	Ask students to break the word at the ending and decode the root word. Teach harder words (with spelling changes) later.	Easy: *jogs* Harder: *jogging*
Two-syllable compound words	Ask students to break the word into two smaller words and decode those words.	Easy: *hotdog* Harder: *doghouse*
Prefixes, such as: • un- (*not, opposite*) • pre- (*before*) • re- (*again, back*)	Tell students the meaning of the prefix and ask them to decode the root word.	*undo* *unlock* *preheat* *pretest* *revise* *reverse*
Suffixes, such as: • -er and -est (comparison) • -er and -or (person who) • -ful (full of)	Tell students the meaning of the suffix and ask them to decode the root word.	*faster, fastest* *teacher, actor* *joyful* *useful*

(Based on Manyak et al., 2018)

Principles of Great Chunking Instruction: Blending Syllabication and Morphology

I now return to the principles of all great foundational skills instruction with a focus on chunking.

1 Explicitly and Systematically Teach Syllabication and Morphology

In research on syllabication (e.g., Bhattacharya & Ehri, 2004; Moats, 2004) and morphology (e.g., Goodwin & Ahn, 2013), instruction includes an explicit, systematic approach. By second grade, you should be developing children's awareness of word parts. Ideally, for your own instruction, pick multisyllabic words that contain syllables or root words that children can decode (e.g., Vadasy et al., 2006). The scope and sequence for this work is not as clear as it is for other forms of sound-spelling instruction. However, broadly, it should include:

- Inflectional morphemes (e.g., -er, -ed, -ing)
- Compound words (e.g., *bathtub*, *hometown*)
- Highly stable syllable patterns such as VC|CV (e.g., *rabbit*, *dinner*, *lesson*)
- High-utility derivational morphemes (e.g., *un-*, *re-*, *-ful*)

2 Use Efficient and Effective Routines

Whereas your decoding routines may work with the whole class, small groups, and individuals, your chunking routines may work best with small groups because children will have even more varied needs. That said, they don't need to take hours a day if you form groups strategically, based on what you know about your students' needs. Try this routine for supporting children in morphology—specifically, how to read words with affixes.

DECODING ROUTINES

Step 1	• Introduce the goal of the routine—for example, "We're going to read words with prefixes. A prefix appears at the beginning of a word. It tells us something about what the word means. A prefix helps us read a word because we can chunk it off, decode it and the root word, and then blend them together. Today's prefix is /re/. /re/ is spelled *r-e* and means 'again.' Say /re/." • On the board or chart, write a word with the target affix, such as *recall*, and read it.

Step 2	• Show or give children words with the target affix to read, such as *reuse*, *reduce*, and *recycle*.
	
	• Show children how to use PQRST to analyze the word. First, write a word with the target affix on the chart or board. Then, follow this procedure:
	
	  P: Tell students to look for a prefix. Circle the prefix. Write the prefix's meaning under it.
	
	  QR: Tell students to look for the "queen root," or the root word. Underline the queen root. Write the root's meaning under it.
	
	  S: Tell students to look for any suffixes. Draw a box around any suffix. Write the suffix's meaning under it.
	
	  T: Ask students to tie all these parts together. Have them pronounce the word and then talk about its definition based on the meanings of the parts that you wrote.
	
	• Repeat with 3–5 words.

Step 3	• Read aloud a word with the target affix. Have children spell the word. • Repeat with 3–5 words.
Step 4	Pick one: • Have children come up with more words that have the target affix. • Pick a queen root in one of the words you studied and come up with affixes that transform it into a different multisyllabic word.

(Based on Goodwin et al., 2012)

3 Respond to the Specific Needs of Children Based on Assessment

Children are more likely to be successful at multisyllabic word reading if they can decode chunks based on their sound-spelling knowledge. While children don't need to know every single possible sound-spelling pattern before attempting multisyllabic words, they should demonstrate reasonable proficiency in single-syllable decoding and, hopefully, evidence of fluency with single-syllable words before diving too deeply into multisyllabic word work. As children learn more about syllables and morphemes, pay attention to those who have difficulty separating words into chunks or putting those chunks back together, especially toward the end of second grade. Check in on their single-syllable decoding first, and then, if necessary, offer them extra practice in regular, two-syllable words, including compound words made up of two CVC words such as *catfish* and *Batman*.

4 Support Chunking With Other Foundational Skills and in Real Reading Contexts

Like all foundational skills, we need to support children in using these skills in context. Books for young children offer lots of opportunities for multisyllabic word reading. *The Adventures of Captain Underpants* is a perfect example!

To support children in chunking words while reading, be clear about what you want them to do. As they're reading, use prompts such as "Do you see a part in this word that you know?" and "Let's find the root word and affixes." Show them how to divide the word into syllables or morphemes and, from there, use your typical decoding prompts to help children make their way through each chunk and then blend them together to identify the word.

Consider Multiple Approaches, Not Just One

This instructional swap is a little different from the earlier ones. Instead of encouraging you to focus on any one approach to chunking, I'm encouraging you to focus on multiple approaches—and strategically choosing among them. The evidence for multisyllabic word reading points toward flexibility (e.g., Bhattacharya, 2020). You might support readers who are ready (likely late first graders and second graders) to notice and use syllable divisions, root words, and affixes to read and spell new words. Or you might encourage children to chunk words into decodable parts by looking for reasonable syllable divisions or affixes they know. In some cases, multiple approaches will get children to the same answer. But in other cases, only one approach will be likely to. Be sure your students know that even though reading multisyllabic words may take a bit more knowledge and effort decoding single-syllable words, it still requires them to use what they've learned about sound-spelling patterns.

> **Do It Tomorrow!**
>
> No matter what grade level you work with, you can infuse a little multisyllabic work into your day tomorrow. Breaking out of foundational skills instruction, you can use a little morphology to deepen vocabulary instruction during a vocabulary-focused read-aloud, science experience, or social studies lesson.
>
> If you are introducing a multimorphemic word with parts that children can easily use to determine meaning (think of words like *sunlight* or *redo*, not words like *repeat*), show children how to chunk the word by morphemes and learn the meaning of the word. This can help children begin to have an awareness that word parts can carry meanings.

Bringing It Together

Chunking isn't as hot as decoding, but it should be. Of the myriad skills required for children to read all kinds of words in the English language, chunking with syllables and morphemes is the one that will enable them to unlock multisyllabic words (Bhattacharya, 2020). Because children will encounter more multisyllabic words, and more complex multisyllabic words, as they make their way through school (Kearns et al., 2016), preparing them to decode and chunk those types of words in the early years is critical.

FLUENCY AND BEYOND

- A child getting phonemic awareness instruction in third grade is finally able to fluently read words and then whole texts.
- Small groups of children are receiving high-quality foundational skills instruction over the summer and are making remarkable gains in accuracy and automaticity.
- Children across elementary classrooms are creating and participating in readers' theater performances, demonstrating highly expressive, fluent reading.

These are just a few scenarios from my own classroom and classrooms I've visited in my work. Foundational skills proficiency opens the door to fluent reading, and fluent reading opens the door to a great number of whole-text experiences. That is the goal of foundational skills instruction. We don't want decoders or chunkers or *phun phonics phact machines*. We want fluent, engaged, and confident readers—readers who focus their energies on comprehension.

As children's word-reading skills develop and they add more and more words to their sight word vocabulary (remember that sight words are words that readers can accurately recognize automatically because they've stored them in long-term memory [Ehri, 2020]), their reading becomes more fluent. This likely means they can devote a greater proportion of their working memory to understanding more and more complex texts as word recognition becomes essentially effortless (e.g., Logan, 1997).

What Is Fluency and Why Is It Important?

Fluency is reading accurately and automatically, and with prosody. In other, less technical words, reading like an exuberant kindergarten teacher sharing *Pinkalicious* with her class! In many ways, fluency is the result of mastery of other foundational skills. These foundational skills, such as word decoding and phonemic awareness, predict reading fluency (Hulme & Snowling, 2015). In the past nine chapters, I've discussed how to support children in accurate and automatic word reading. The culmination of these skills, along with prosody, is fluent reading.

Like all foundational skills, fluency all by itself should not be our goal. We want children to become fluent readers because it supports reading comprehension. We know this from studies that investigate the connections between fluency and comprehension in several ways:

- Interventions and curricula designed to improve fluency can also improve comprehension (Therrien et al., 2006).
- Children who demonstrate less fluency tend to have difficulties in comprehension (Álvarez-Cañizo et al., 2015; Sabatini et al., 2019; White et al., 2021).
- Reading fluency at one time predicts reading comprehension later (Lepola et al., 2016; Torppa et al., 2016).

Fluent reading supports reading comprehension, the goal of our foundational skills and comprehension instruction.

Fluency, as I've mentioned above, is three elements: accurate word reading, automatic word reading, and prosody. The first two elements, accurate and automatic word reading, are the result of decoding and generating orthographic maps. A child who is fluently reading a text has moved beyond decoding the words in that text. They've stored these words in their long-term memory and are effortlessly reading each word.

Prosody—or the reader's expression and all its components: timing, phrasing, intonation, rhythm—is often left out of conversations about fluency but is beginning to be more recognized by researchers. It is highly related to comprehension, even in early elementary school (Godde et al., 2020; Wolters et al., 2020). It is thought to be related to comprehension for several reasons (Wolters et al., 2020): 1) it might help readers hold phrases in memory; 2) it may be a result of or indicator of comprehension in the moment; and 3) it might be a result of understanding print concepts and syntax. Like all aspects of fluency, prosody is a culmination of skills. When thinking about fluency, it is essential to think beyond fast and accurate word recognition. We need to encourage children to also read with appropriate expression for the genre, text, and meaning.

Fluency might matter more for comprehension as children enter later elementary school. Some studies find a weaker relationship between fluency and comprehension in early grades than the relationship seen in later elementary grades (Schwanenflugel et al., 2004). This makes sense because a child still learning to decode words is unlikely to demonstrate fluency in most texts. Therefore, they are not going to read words accurately or automatically. In these early grades, it is also unlikely that children will demonstrate much prosody (Godde et al., 2020). These realities of development might make us think we shouldn't worry about fluency at all until children have mastered decoding. However, we can support children's emergent fluency by thinking about a combination of modeling and the right types of texts.

ESSENTIAL INSTRUCTIONAL SWAP

Less Fluency as Speed Reading, More Holistic Fluency

Fluency, unlike the other foundational skills, does not lend itself as readily to our four principles of great instruction. Because it requires a combination of many skills, we are better served by thinking more holistically about fluency.

Many instructional recommendations for fluency are essentially recommendations for speed reading. This may support children in accelerating their pace and, especially in repeated readings, may support accuracy and automaticity (e.g., Lee & Yoon, 2017). Instead of thinking about fluency just in terms of speed, we need to consider more about children's experiences with individual texts and prosody.

I am a fluent reader, yet I cannot read everything fluently. Presented with a scientific article about a new medical procedure, I doubt I would demonstrate much fluency. It's important that we recognize this with our students as well. While we can aim for children to be fluent readers of any text, fluency is really a function of a reader's interaction with a specific text.

In the early years, we know children tend to read more fluently when given texts:

- with lots of high-frequency words (Compton et al., 2004)
- with repeated words or word parts (Hiebert & Fisher, 2016)
- with familiar words (Williams & Morris, 2004)
- with a high proportion of decodable words (Mesmer, 2005)
- related to prior knowledge (Priebe et al., 2012)

We also know that children tend to have greater fluency in narrative texts and read more slowly in informational texts (Tortorelli, 2019). When we think about supporting and assessing fluency, we need to be aware of the features of the texts we put in front of children. We want to give children texts they are appropriately challenged by, but also that they can succeed within. When having children practice fluency, be sure to select texts that enable them to do so. By the same token, if you choose to assess oral reading fluency, evaluate the text you choose. Audit the text to ensure it is not privileging certain background knowledge or words that may be more familiar to some students.

As described above, we also need to be aware of how we support and encourage prosody in children's reading. Focus on modeling prosody in your read-alouds and shared reading. You should also encourage children to practice appropriate expression and intonation during repeated readings.

To learn more about teaching fluency and for many, many instructional ideas, I suggest *The Megabook of Fluency: Strategies and Texts to Engage All Readers* by Timothy V. Rasinski and Melissa Cheesman Smith.

Bringing It Together

There may be nothing more gratifying than supporting a child who knows very little about the alphabet all the way through foundational skills toward fluent reading. Listening to them, for the first time, gracefully sail through the words of a new book, feels magical. Though we feel the magic, and they likely do, too, though we can acknowledge the inexplicable wonder of moments like this, the truth is: Learning reading isn't magic. Learning to read words takes incredible effort. It takes incredible teaching. It takes careful application of foundational skills in concert.

To create fluent readers, we must first think back to each foundational skill and its importance in our work. Oral language, print concepts, phonemic awareness, alphabet knowledge, sound-spelling knowledge, decoding, syllabication, morphological awareness, and chunking enable fluency. Gaps in skills or knowledge across any of these might prevent a child from becoming a proficient reader. To prevent this, we return to the four principles of what all great foundational skills instruction should be:

1. **Explicit and systematic** Teach all the skills with clear, straightforward language. Don't leave learning to chance.

2. **Efficient and effective** Use routines that are fast *and* powerful. Spend your time in foundations wisely to free up more time for specific needs and deeper comprehension work.

3. **Responsive to children's needs** All children are different and will have varied needs. Differentiate your instruction when possible to directly meet their specific needs to successfully read words.

4. **Integrated with and applied to real reading and writing** Foundational skills are a means to an end. They only matter because we need them to engage in real reading and writing related to our interests, knowledge, and new learnings. Always ensure children feel this connection.

Throughout this book, I moved from introducing the basics of our written system to single-syllable word decoding to multisyllabic word chunking. I grounded my discussion in research, in how humans read, and in practical ways to implement science-backed practices in classrooms. This is how you can guide your students toward fluency, of individual texts and across many texts: by purposefully teaching them what they need to know about words, by helping them discover the joy and magic in decoding and chunking, and by grounding yourself and your students in the art and science of reading instruction.

To create fluent readers, we must first think back to each foundational skill and its importance in our work. Oral language, print concepts, phonemic awareness, alphabet knowledge, sound-spelling knowledge, decoding, syllabication, morphological awareness, and chunking enable fluency.

A CALL TO ACTION

Disagreements about how to teach reading never seem to end. And we may never find a "silver bullet" for reading instruction, because, in all likelihood, there isn't one. As Twitter continues to flash controversial messages about reading, remember we can draw upon and learn from quality research and practice. Focus on what we know works. Focus on purposefully guiding children to decode words, chunk words, and—most of all—read fluently, proficiently, and joyfully.

That doesn't mean you shouldn't engage in conversations about reading. In fact, to me, it means being completely engaged—engaged in conversations with colleagues, engaged in the latest, most reliable ideas about teaching reading, and engaged in your instruction by observing closely what your students are doing as they read. I hope you continue to read about best practices and learn from others for the rest of your career. Research and practice are constantly innovating, leading us down paths that will undoubtedly help us find even better ways to teach our young readers.

So, what will you try tomorrow? What will you aim for this month? Envision the readers you want to create in your classroom, above the noise, above the confusion, above the fray.

We can draw upon and learn from quality research and practice. Focus on what we know works. Focus on purposefully guiding children to decode words, chunk words, and—most of all—read fluently, proficiently, and joyfully.

REFERENCES

Álvarez-Cañizo, M., Suárez-Coalla, P., & Cuetos, F. (2015). The role of reading fluency in children's text comprehension. *Frontiers in Psychology, 6*, 1810.

Amendum, S. J., Conradi, K., & Hiebert, E. (2018). Does text complexity matter in the elementary grades? A research synthesis of text difficulty and elementary students' reading fluency and comprehension. *Educational Psychology Review, 30*(1), 121–151.

Anthony, J. L., & Francis, D. J. (2005). Development of phonological awareness. *Current Directions in Psychological Science, 14*(5), 255–259.

August, D., Uccelli, P., Artzi, L., Barr, C., & Francis, D. J. (2020). English learners' acquisition of academic vocabulary: Instruction matters, but so do word characteristics. *Reading Research Quarterly.*

Austin, C. R., Vaughn, S., Clemens, N. H., Pustejovsky, J. E., & Boucher, A. N. (2021). The relative effects of instruction linking word reading and word meaning compared to word reading instruction alone on the accuracy, fluency, and word meaning knowledge of 4th-5th grade students with dyslexia. *Scientific Studies of Reading*, 1–19.

Beck, I. L., McKeown, M. G., & Kucan, L. (2013). *Bringing words to life: Robust vocabulary instruction.* New York: Guilford Press.

Becker, R., & Sylvan, L. (2021). Coupling articulatory placement strategies with phonemic awareness instruction to support emergent literacy skills in preschool children: A collaborative approach. *Language, Speech, and Hearing Services in Schools, 52*(2), 661–674.

Bell, Y. R., & Clark, T. R. (1998). Culturally relevant reading material as related to comprehension and recall in African American children. *Journal of Black Psychology, 24*(4), 455–475.

Bhattacharya, A., & Ehri, L. C. (2004). Graphosyllabic analysis helps adolescent struggling readers read and spell words. *Journal of Learning Disabilities, 37*(4), 331–348.

Bhattacharya, A. (2020). Syllabic versus morphemic analyses: Teaching multisyllabic word reading to older struggling readers. *Journal of Adolescent & Adult Literacy, 63*(5), 491–497.

Bogan, B. L. (2012). Decodable and predictable texts: Forgotten resources to teach the beginning reader. *International Journal of Arts and Commerce, 1*(6), 1–8.

Bowey, J. A., & Muller, D. (2005). Phonological recoding and rapid orthographic learning in third-graders' silent reading: A critical test of the self-teaching hypothesis. *Journal of Experimental Child Psychology, 92*(3), 203–219.

Boyer, N., & Ehri, L. C. (2011). Contribution of phonemic segmentation instruction with letters and articulation pictures to word reading and spelling in beginners. *Scientific Studies of Reading, 15*(5), 440–470.

Brady, S. (2021). Key components for beginners: Letter knowledge, phoneme awareness, and handwriting. *Learning Ally.* https://learningally.org/Solutions-for-School/Educator-Blog/key-components-for-beginners-knowledge-phoneme-awareness-and-handwriting

Brown, K. J., Patrick, K. C., Fields, M. K., & Craig, G. T. (2021). Phonological awareness materials in Utah kindergartens: A case study in the science of reading. *Reading Research Quarterly, 56*, S249–S272.

Buckingham, J. (2020). Systematic phonics instruction belongs in evidence-based reading programs: A response to Bowers, *Educational and Developmental Psychologist*, 37:2, 105-113, DOI: 10.1017/edp.2020.12

Bus, A. G., & van IJzendoorn, M. H. (1999). Phonological awareness and early reading: A meta-analysis of experimental training studies. *Journal of Educational Psychology, 91*(3), 403.

Cain, K., & Oakhill, J. (2011). Matthew effects in young readers: Reading comprehension and reading experience aid vocabulary development. *Journal of Learning Disabilities, 44*(5), 431–443.

Caravolas, M., Lervåg, A., Mikulajová, M., Defior, S., Seidlová-Málková, G., & Hulme, C. (2019). A cross-linguistic, longitudinal study of the foundations of decoding and reading comprehension ability. *Scientific Studies of Reading, 23*(5), 386–402.

Cartledge, G., Keesey, S., Bennett, J. G., Ramnath, R., & Council III, M. R. (2016). Culturally relevant literature: What matters most to primary-age urban learners. *Reading & Writing Quarterly, 32*(5), 399–426.

Center for Black Educator Development (2020). *Demonstrating the power of freedom: Virtual Freedom Schools Literacy Academy 2020 impact report card.* https://static1.squarespace.com/static/5df3f23a2e878f341fa14f7a/t/604b8b26774edd081bdba2af/1615563573753/%5BCBED%5D-FSLA-Scorecard.pdf

Chambré, S. J., Ehri, L. C., & Ness, M. (2020). Phonological decoding enhances orthographic facilitation of vocabulary learning in first graders. *Reading and Writing, 33*(5), 1133–1162.

Cheatham, J. P., & Allor, J. H. (2012). The influence of decodability in early reading text on reading achievement: A review of the evidence. *Reading and Writing, 25*(9), 2223–2246.

Christensen, C. A., & Bowey, J. A. (2005). The efficacy of orthographic rime, grapheme–phoneme correspondence, and implicit phonics approaches to teaching decoding skills. *Scientific Studies of Reading, 9*(4), 327–349.

Chu, M. C., & Chen, S. H. (2014). Comparison of the effects of two phonics training programs on L2 word reading. *Psychological Reports, 114*(1), 272–291.

Clay, M. M. (1968). A syntactic analysis of reading errors. *Journal of Verbal Learning and Verbal Behavior, 7*(2), 434–438.

Clay, M. (2017). *Concepts about print: What has a child learned about the way we print language?* Second edition. Portsmouth, NH: Heinemann.

Clayton, F. J., West, G., Sears, C., Hulme, C., & Lervåg, A. (2020). A longitudinal study of early reading development: letter-sound knowledge, phoneme awareness and RAN, but not letter-sound integration, predict variations in reading development. *Scientific Studies of Reading, 24*(2), 91–107.

Clemens, N., Solari, E., Kearns, D. M., Fien, H., Nelson, N. J., Stelega, M., ... Hoeft, F. (2021). They say you can do phonemic awareness instruction "in the dark," but should you? A critical evaluation of the trend toward advanced phonemic awareness training. https://doi.org/10.31234/osf.io/ajxbv

Compton, D. L., Appleton, A. C., & Hosp, M. K. (2004). Exploring the relationship between text-leveling systems and reading accuracy and fluency in second-grade students who are average and poor readers. *Learning Disabilities Research and Practice, 19*, 176–184.

Cunningham, A. E., Perry, K. E., Stanovich, K. E., & Share, D. L. (2002). Orthographic learning during reading: Examining the role of self-teaching. *Journal of Experimental Child Psychology, 82*(3), 185–199.

Cunningham, P. M., & Cunningham, J. W. (1992). Making words: Enhancing the invented spelling-decoding connection. *The Reading Teacher, 46*(2), 106–115.

de Graaff, S., Bosman, A. M., Hasselman, F., & Verhoeven, L. (2009). Benefits of systematic phonics instruction. *Scientific Studies of Reading, 13*(4), 318–333.

Dessemontet, R. S., Martinet, C., de Chambrier, A. F., Martini-Willemin, B. M., & Audrin, C. (2019). A meta-analysis on the effectiveness of phonics instruction for teaching decoding skills to students with intellectual disability. *Educational Research Review, 26,* 52–70.

Duke, N. K. (2020). When readers get stuck: There's an art—and science—to providing prompts for young readers when they struggle. *Educational Leadership, 78*(3), 26–33.

Duke, N. K., & Cartwright, K. B. (2021). The science of reading progresses: Communicating advances beyond the simple view of reading. *Reading Research Quarterly, 56,* S25–S44.

Duke, N. K. Ward, A., & Klingelhofer, R. (2020). Listening to reading; Watching while writing protocol. https://www.nellkduke.org/listening-to-reading-protocol

Duke, N. K., & Mesmer, H. A. E. (2018). Phonics faux pas: Avoiding instructional missteps in teaching letter-sound relationships. *American Educator, 42*(4), 12-16. https://www.aft.org/ae/winter2018-2019/duke_mesmer

Duke, N. K., Norman, R. R., Roberts, K. L., Martin, N. M., Knight, J. A., Morsink, P. M., & Calkins, S. L. (2013). Beyond concepts of print: Development of concepts of graphics in text, pre-K to grade 3. *Research in the Teaching of English, 48,* 175–203.

Duncan, L. G., & Seymour, P. H. (2003). How do children read multisyllabic words? Some preliminary observations. *Journal of Research in Reading, 26*(2), 101–120.

Ehri, L. C., & Flugman, B. (2018). Mentoring teachers in systematic phonics instruction: Effectiveness of an intensive year-long program for kindergarten through 3rd grade teachers and their students. *Reading and Writing, 31*(2), 425–456.

Ehri, L. C. (2005). Learning to read words: Theory, findings, and issues. *Scientific Studies of Reading, 9*(2), 167-188.

Ehri, L. C. (2014). Orthographic mapping in the acquisition of sight word reading, spelling memory, and vocabulary learning. *Scientific Studies of Reading, 18*(1), 5–21.

Ehri, L. C. (2020). The science of learning to read words: A case for systematic phonics instruction. *Reading Research Quarterly, 55,* S45–S60.

Eldredge, J. L., Reutzel, D. R., & Hollingsworth, P. M. (1996). Comparing the effectiveness of two oral reading practices: Round-robin reading and the shared book experience. *Journal of Literacy Research, 28*(2), 201–225.

Elkonin, D. B. (1963). The psychology of mastering the elements of reading. *Educational Psychology in the USSR,* 165–179.

Erbeli, F., & Rice, M. (2021). Examining the effects of silent independent reading on reading outcomes: A narrative synthesis review from 2000 to 2020. *Reading & Writing Quarterly,* 1–19.

Fien, H., Smith, J. L., Smolkowski, K., Baker, S. K., Nelson, N. J., & Chaparro, E. (2015). An examination of the efficacy of a multitiered intervention on early reading outcomes for first grade students at risk for reading difficulties. *Journal of Learning Disabilities, 48*(6), 602–621.

Foorman, B., Beyler, N., Borradaile, K., Coyne, M., Denton, C. A., Dimino, J., & Wissel, S. (2016). Foundational skills to support reading for understanding in kindergarten through 3rd grade. *Educator's Practice Guide.* NCEE 2016-4008. What Works Clearinghouse.

Fulmer, S. M., & Frijters, J. C. (2011). Motivation during an excessively challenging reading task: The buffering role of relative topic interest. The *Journal of Experimental Education, 79*(2), 185–208.

Gay, G. (2010). *Culturally responsive teaching: Theory, research, and practice.* New York: Teachers College Press.

Gellert, A. S., Arnbak, E., Wischmann, S., & Elbro, C. (2021). Morphological intervention for students with limited vocabulary knowledge: Short- and long-term transfer effects. *Reading Research Quarterly.*

Godde, E., Bosse, M. L., & Bailly, G. (2020). A review of reading prosody acquisition and development. *Reading and Writing, 33*(2), 399–426.

Gonzalez-Frey, S. M., & Ehri, L. C. (2021). Connected phonation is more effective than segmented phonation for teaching beginning readers to decode unfamiliar words. *Scientific Studies of Reading, 25*(3), 272–285.

Goodman, K. S. (1970). Psycholinguistic universals in the reading process. *Visible Language, 4*(2), 103–110.

Goodwin, A. P., & Ahn, S. (2010). A meta-analysis of morphological interventions: Effects on literacy achievement of children with literacy difficulties. *Annals of Dyslexia, 60*(2), 183–208.

Goodwin, A. P., & Ahn, S. (2013). A meta-analysis of morphological interventions in English: Effects on literacy outcomes for school-age children. *Scientific Studies of Reading, 17*(4), 257–285.

Goodwin, A., Lipsky, M., & Ahn, S. (2012). Word detectives: Using units of meaning to support literacy. *The Reading Teacher, 65*(7), 461–470.

Gough, P. B., & Tunmer, W. E. (1986). Decoding, reading, and reading disability. *Remedial and Special Education, 7*(1), 6–10.

Grainger, J. (2008). Cracking the orthographic code: An introduction. *Language and Cognitive Processes, 23*(1), 1–35.

Grainger, J. (2018). Orthographic processing: A "mid-level" vision of reading: The 44th Sir Frederic Bartlett Lecture. *Quarterly Journal of Experimental Psychology, 71*(2), 335–359.

Gray, S. H., Ehri, L. C., & Locke, J. L. (2018). Morpho-phonemic analysis boosts word reading for adult struggling readers. *Reading and Writing, 31*(1), 75–98

Hammill, D. D. (2004). What we know about correlates of reading. *Exceptional Children, 70*(4), 453–469.

Hammond, Z. (2014). *Culturally responsive teaching and the brain: Promoting authentic engagement and rigor among culturally and linguistically diverse students.* Thousand Oaks, CA: Corwin Press.

Hanna, P. R. (1966). Phoneme-grapheme correspondences as cues to spelling improvement. Office of Education, Department of Health, Education, and Welfare.

Hatcher, P. J., & Hulme, C. (1999). Phonemes, rhymes, and intelligence as predictors of children's responsiveness to remedial reading instruction: Evidence from a longitudinal intervention study. *Journal of Experimental Child Psychology, 72*(2), 130–153.

Hatcher, P. J., Hulme, C., & Snowling, M. J. (2004). Explicit phoneme training combined with phonic reading instruction helps young children at risk of reading failure. *Journal of Child Psychology and Psychiatry, 45*(2), 338–358.

Heggie, L., & Wade-Woolley, L. (2017). Reading longer words: Insights into multisyllabic word reading. *Perspectives of the ASHA Special Interest Groups, 2*(1), 86–94.

Henbest, V. S., & Apel, K. (2017). Effective word reading instruction: What does the evidence tell us? *Communication Disorders Quarterly, 39*(1), 303–311.

Hernandez, D. J. (2011). *Double jeopardy: How third-grade reading skills and poverty influence high school graduation.* Annie E. Casey Foundation.

Hiebert, E., & Fisher, C. (2016). A comparison of the effects of two phonetically regular text types on young English learners' literacy. *Reading Research Report,* 16–01.

Honchell, B., & Schulz, M. (2012). Engaging young readers with text through shared experiences. *Journal of Inquiry and Action in Education, 4*(3), 59–67.

Huang, F. L., Tortorelli, L. S., & Invernizzi, M. A. (2014). An investigation of factors associated with letter-sound knowledge at kindergarten entry. *Early Childhood Research Quarterly, 29*(2), 182–192.

Hulme, C., & Snowling, M. J. (2015). Learning to read: What we know and what we need to understand better. *Child Development Perspectives, 7*(1), 1–5.

Javorsky, K. H. (2014). *Digital print concepts: Conceptualizing a modern framework for measuring emerging knowledge.* The University of Nebraska-Lincoln.

Jones, C. D., Clark, S. K., & Reutzel, D. R. (2013). Enhancing alphabet knowledge instruction: Research implications and practical strategies for early childhood educators. *Early Childhood Education Journal, 41*(2), 81–89.

Juel, C., & Minden-Cupp, C. (2000). Learning to read words: Linguistic units and instructional strategies. *Reading Research Quarterly, 35*(4), 458–492.

Juel, C., & Roper-Schneider, D. (1985). The influence of basal readers on first grade reading. *Reading Research Quarterly,* 134–152.

Juel, C., Griffith, P. L., & Gough, P. B. (1986). Acquisition of literacy: A longitudinal study of children in first and second grade. *Journal of Educational Psychology, 78,* 243–255.

Justice, L. M., & Ezell, H. K. (2002). Use of storybook reading to increase print awareness in at-risk children. *American Journal of Speech-language Pathology, 11*(1), 17–29.

Justice, L. M., Skibbe, L., Canning, A., & Lankford, C. (2005). Pre-schoolers, print and storybooks: An observational study using eye movement analysis. *Journal of Research in Reading, 28*(3), 229–243.

Justice, L. M., McGinty, A. S., Cabell, S. Q., Kilday, C. R., Knighton, K., & Huffman, G. (2010). Language and literacy curriculum supplement for preschoolers who are academically at risk: A feasibility study. *Language, Speech, and Hearing Services in Schools, 41,* 161–178.

Kearns, D. M. (2020). Does English have useful syllable division patterns? *Reading Research Quarterly, 55,* S145–S160.

Kearns, D. M., Steacy, L. M., Compton, D. L., Gilbert, J. K., Goodwin, A. P., Cho, E., ... & Collins, A. A. (2016). Modeling polymorphemic word recognition: Exploring differences among children with early-emerging and late-emerging word reading difficulty. *Journal of Learning Disabilities, 49*(4), 368–394.

Kearns, D. M. (2015). How elementary-age children read polysyllabic polymorphemic words. *Journal of Educational Psychology, 107*(2), 364.

Keesey, S., Konrad, M., & Joseph, L. M. (2015). Word boxes improve phonemic awareness, letter–sound correspondences, and spelling skills of at-risk kindergartners. *Remedial and Special Education, 36*(3), 167–180.

Kenner, B. B., Terry, N. P., Friehling, A. H., & Namy, L. L. (2017). Phonemic awareness development in 2.5- and 3.5-year-old children: An examination of emergent, receptive, knowledge and skills. *Reading and Writing, 30*(7), 1575–1594.

Kilpatrick, D. A. (2015). *Essentials of assessing, preventing, and overcoming reading difficulties.* Hoboken, NJ: John Wiley & Sons.

Ladson-Billings, G. (1995). Toward a theory of culturally relevant pedagogy. *American Educational Research Journal, 32*(3), 465–491.

Landerl, K., & Wimmer, H. (2008). Development of word reading fluency and spelling in a consistent orthography: An 8-year follow-up. *Journal of Educational Psychology, 100*(1), 150.

Lee, J., & Yoon, S. Y. (2017). The effects of repeated reading on reading fluency for students with reading disabilities: A meta-analysis. *Journal of Learning Disabilities, 50*(2), 213–224.

Lefebvre, P., Trudeau, N., & Sutton, A. (2011). Enhancing vocabulary, print awareness and phonological awareness through shared storybook reading with low-income preschoolers. *Journal of Early Childhood Literacy, 11*(4), 453–479.

Lepola, J., Lynch, J., Kiuru, N., Laakkonen, E., & Niemi, P. (2016). Early oral language comprehension, task orientation, and foundational reading skills as predictors of grade 3 reading comprehension. *Reading Research Quarterly, 51*(4), 373–390.

Leppänen, U., Aunola, K., Niemi, P., & Nurmi, J. E. (2008). Letter knowledge predicts Grade 4 reading fluency and reading comprehension. *Learning and Instruction, 18*(6), 548–564.

Lervåg, A., Hulme, C., & Melby-Lervåg, M. (2018). Unpicking the developmental relationship between oral language skills and reading comprehension: It's simple, but complex. *Child Development, 89*(5), 1821–1838.

Levy, B. A., Gong, Z., Hessels, S., Evans, M. A., & Jared, D. (2006). Understanding print: Early reading development and the contributions of home literacy experiences. *Journal of Experimental Child Psychology, 93*(1), 6–93.

Lindsey, J. (2021). *Realigning early reading instruction with research: A preliminary evaluation of two research-based early reading programs* (Doctoral dissertation, University of Michigan). ProQuest Dissertations.

Logan, G. D. (1997). Automaticity and reading: Perspectives from the instance theory of automatization. *Reading & Writing Quarterly: Overcoming Learning Difficulties, 13*(2), 123–146.

Lovett, M. W., Lacerenza, L., & Borden, S. L. (2000). Putting struggling readers on the PHAST track: A program to integrate phonological and strategy-based remedial reading instruction and maximize outcomes. *Journal of Learning Disabilities, 33*(5), 458–476.

Manyak, P., Baumann, J., & Manyak, A. (2018). Morphological analysis instruction in the elementary grades: Which morphemes to teach and how to teach them. *The Reading Teacher, 72,* 289–300.

Mesmer, H. A. E., & Lake, K. (2010). The role of syllable awareness and syllable-controlled text in the development of finger-point reading. *Reading Psychology, 31*(2), 176–201.

Mesmer, H. A. E., & Williams, T. O. (2015). Examining the role of syllable awareness in a model of concept of word: Findings from preschoolers. *Reading Research Quarterly, 50*(4), 483–497.

Mesmer, H. A. E. (2005). Text decodability and the first-grade reader. *Reading & Writing Quarterly, 21,* 61–86.

Michaud, M., Dion, E., Barrette, A., Dupéré, V., & Toste, J. (2017). Does knowing what a word means influence how easily its decoding is learned?. *Reading & Writing Quarterly, 33*(1), 82–96.

Miles, K. P., & Ehri, L. C. (2019). Orthographic mapping facilitates sight word memory and vocabulary learning. In *Reading Development and Difficulties* (pp. 63–82). Springer, Cham.

Moats, L. (2009). Knowledge foundations for teaching reading and spelling. *Reading and Writing, 22*(4), 379–399.

Moats, L. (2000) *Speech to print: Language essentials for teachers.* Baltimore, MD: Paul H. Brookes Pub.

Moats, L. C. (2004). Efficacy of a structured, systematic language curriculum for adolescent poor readers. *Reading & Writing Quarterly, 20*(2), 145–159.

Mol, S. E., Bus, A. G., & de Jong, M. T. (2009). Interactive book reading in early education: A tool to stimulate print knowledge as well as oral language. *Review of Educational Research, 79,* 979–1007.

Møller, H. L., Mortensen, J. O., & Elbro, C. (2021). Effects of integrated spelling in phonics instruction for at-risk children in kindergarten. *Reading & Writing Quarterly,* 1–16.

Morrison, K. A., Robbins, H. H., & Rose, D. G. (2008). Operationalizing culturally relevant pedagogy: A synthesis of classroom-based research. *Equity & Excellence in Education, 41*(4), 433–452.

Müller, B., Richter, T., & Karageorgos, P. (2020). Syllable-based reading improvement: Effects on word reading and reading comprehension in Grade 2. *Learning and Instruction, 66,* 101304.

Muncer, S. J., & Knight, D. C. (2012). The bigram trough hypothesis and the syllable number effect in lexical decision. *Quarterly Journal of Experimental Psychology, 65*(11), 2221–2230.

Muter, V., Hulme, C., Snowling, M., & Taylor, S. (1998). Segmentation, not rhyming, predicts early progress in learning to read. *Journal of Experimental Child Psychology, 71*(1), 3–27.

NAEP Reading Report Card. (2019). Retrieved from https://nces.ed.gov/nationsreportcard/

Nagy, W. E., & Anderson, R. C. (1984). How many words are there in printed school English? *Reading Research Quarterly*, 304–330.

Nation, K., & Hulme, C. (1997). Phonemic segmentation, not onset-rime segmentation, predicts early reading and spelling skills. *Reading Research Quarterly, 32*(2), 154–167.

Nation, K., & Hulme, C. (2011). Learning to read changes children's phonological skills: Evidence from a latent variable longitudinal study of reading and nonword repetition. *Developmental Science, 14*(4), 649–659.

Nation, K., Angell, P., & Castles, A. (2007). Orthographic learning via self-teaching in children learning to read English: Effects of exposure, durability, and context. *Journal of Experimental Child Psychology, 96*(1), 71–84.

National Early Literacy Panel (2008). *Developing early Literacy: Report of the National Early Literacy Panel.* Jessup, MD: National Institute for Literacy.

National Reading Panel (2000). *Report of the National Reading Panel: Teaching children to read: An evidence-based assessment of the scientific research literature on reading and its implications for reading instruction: Reports of the subgroups.* Rockville, MD: NICHD Clearinghouse.

Nevo, E., & Vaknin-Nusbaum, V. (2018). Enhancing language and print-concept skills by using interactive storybook reading in kindergarten. *Journal of Early Childhood Literacy, 18*(4), 545–569.

Norman, R. R. (2010). Picture this: Processes prompted by graphics in informational text. *Literacy Teaching and Learning, 14*, 1–39.

O'Connor, R. E., Beach, K. D., Sanchez, V. M., Bocian, K. M., & Flynn, L. J. (2015). Building BRIDGES: A design experiment to improve reading and United States history knowledge of poor readers in eighth grade. *Exceptional Children, 81*, 399–425. https://doi.org/10.177/0014402914563706

Paige, D. D., Smith, G. S., Rasinski, T. V., Rupley, W. H., Magpuri-Lavell, T., & Nichols, W. D. (2019). A path analytic model linking foundational skills to grade 3 state reading achievement. *The Journal of Educational Research, 112*(1), 110–120.

Perfetti, C. A., Beck, I., Bell, L. C., & Hughes, C. (1987). Phonemic knowledge and learning to read are reciprocal: A longitudinal study of first grade children. *Merrill-Palmer Quarterly* (1982-), 283–319.

Perfetti, C. (2007). Reading ability: Lexical quality to comprehension. *Scientific Studies of Reading, 11*(4), 357–383.

Piasta, S. B., & Wagner, R. K. (2010). Developing early literacy skills: A meta-analysis of alphabet learning and instruction. *Reading Research Quarterly, 45*(1), 8–38.

Piasta, S. B., Justice, L. M., McGinty, A. S., & Kaderavek, J. N. (2012). Increasing young children's contact with print during shared reading: Longitudinal effects on literacy achievement. *Child Development, 83*(3), 810–820.

Piper, R. E. (2019). Navigating Black identity development: The power of interactive multicultural read-alouds with elementary-aged children. *Education Sciences, 9*(2), 141.

Pratt, S. M. (2020). A mixed methods approach to exploring the relationship between beginning readers' dialog about their thinking and ability to self-correct oral reading. *Reading Psychology, 41*(1), 1–43.

Priebe, S. J., Keenan, J. M., & Miller, A. C. (2012). How prior knowledge affects word identification and comprehension. *Reading and Writing, 25*(1), 131–149.

Pritchard, S. C., Coltheart, M., Marinus, E., & Castles, A. (2018). A computational model of the self-teaching hypothesis based on the dual-route cascaded model of reading. *Cognitive Science, 42*(3), 722–770.

Pritchard, V. E., Malone, S. A., & Hulme, C. (2021). Early handwriting ability predicts the growth of children's spelling, but not reading, skills. *Scientific Studies of Reading, 25*(4), 304–318.

Puzio, K., Colby, G. T., & Algeo-Nichols, D. (2020). Differentiated literacy instruction: Boondoggle or best practice? *Review of Educational Research, 90*(4), 459–498.

Rastle, K., Lally, C., Davis, M. H., & Taylor, J. S. H. (2021). The dramatic impact of explicit instruction on learning to read in a new writing system. *Psychological Science, 32*(4), 471–484.

Reed, D. K. (2008). A synthesis of morphology interventions and effects on reading outcomes for students in grades K–12. *Learning Disabilities Research & Practice, 23*(1), 36–49.

Rehfeld, D. M. (2021). *Phonemic awareness instruction with children at risk of reading failure* (Doctoral dissertation).

Roberts, T. A. (2021). Learning letters: Evidence and questions from a science-of-reading Perspective. *Reading Research Quarterly, 56*, S171–S192.

Roberts, T. A., Vadasy, P. F., & Sanders, E. A. (2018). Preschoolers' alphabet learning: Letter name and sound instruction, cognitive processes, and English proficiency. *Early Childhood Research Quarterly, 44*, 257–274.

Roberts, T. A., Vadasy, P. F., & Sanders, E. A. (2019). Preschoolers' alphabet learning: Cognitive, teaching sequence, and English proficiency influences. *Reading Research Quarterly, 54*(3), 413–437.

Roberts, T. A., Vadasy, P. F., & Sanders, E. A. (2020). Preschool instruction in letter names and sounds: Does contextualized or decontextualized instruction matter? *Reading Research Quarterly, 55*(4), 573–600.

Roth, F. P., Speece, D. L., & Cooper, D. H. (2002). A longitudinal analysis of the connection between oral language and early reading. *The Journal of Educational Research, 95*(5), 259–272.

Rvachew, S., Rees, K., Carolan, E., & Nadig, A. (2017). Improving emergent literacy with school-based shared reading: Paper versus ebooks. *International Journal of Child-Computer Interaction, 12*, 24–29.

Ryder, R. J., Burton, J. L., & Silberg, A. (2006). Longitudinal study of direct instruction effects from first through third grades. *The Journal of Educational Research, 99*(3), 179–192.

Sabatini, J., Wang, Z., & O'Reilly, T. (2019). Relating reading comprehension to oral reading performance in the NAEP fourth-grade special study of oral reading. *Reading Research Quarterly, 54*(2), 253–271.

Savage, R., & Stuart, M. (1998). Sublexical inferences in beginning reading: Medial vowel digraphs as functional units of transfer. *Journal of Experimental Child Psychology, 69*(2), 85–108.

Scarborough, H. S. (2001). Connecting early language and literacy to later reading (dis)abilities: Evidence, theory, and practice. In S. B. Neuman & D. K. Dickinson (Eds.), *Handbook of early literacy research* (Vol. 1, pp. 97–110). New York: Guilford Press.

Schaars, M. M., Segers, E., & Verhoeven, L. (2017). Word decoding development during phonics instruction in children at risk for dyslexia. *Dyslexia, 23*(2), 141–160.

Schacter, J., & Jo, B. (2005). Learning when school is not in session: a reading summer day-camp intervention to improve the achievement of exiting first-grade students who are economically disadvantaged. *Journal of Research in Reading, 28*(2), 158–169.

Schwanenflugel, P. J., Hamilton, A. M., Kuhn, M. R., Wisenbaker, J. M., & Stahl, S. A. (2004). Becoming a fluent reader: Reading skill and prosodic features in the oral reading of young readers. *Journal of Educational Psychology, 96*(1), 119.

Shamir, A., & Korat, O. (2015). Educational electronic books for supporting emergent literacy of kindergarteners at-risk for reading difficulties—What do we know so far? *Computers in the Schools, 32*(2), 105–121.

Shamir, A., & Shlafer, I. (2011). E-books effectiveness in promoting phonological awareness and concept about print: A comparison between children at risk for learning disabilities and typically developing kindergarteners. *Computers & Education, 57*(3), 1989–1997.

Share, D. L. (1995). Phonological recoding and self-teaching: Sine qua non of reading acquisition. *Cognition, 55*(2), 151–218.

Share, D. L. (2004). Orthographic learning at a glance: On the time course and developmental onset of self-teaching. *Journal of Experimental Child Psychology, 87*(4), 267–298.

Share, D. L. (2008). Orthographic learning, phonological recoding, and self-teaching. In *Advances in Child Development and Behavior* (Vol. 36, pp. 31–82). JAI.

Share, D. L., Jorm, A. F., Maclean, R., & Matthews, R. (1984). Sources of individual differences in reading acquisition. *Journal of Educational Psychology, 76*(6), 1309.

Shipley, K. G., & McAfee, J. G. (2019). *Assessment in speech-language pathology: A resource manual.* Plural Publishing.

Shmidman, A., & Ehri, L. (2010). Embedded picture mnemonics to learn letters. *Scientific Studies of Reading, 14*(2), 159–182.

Silverman, R. D., Johnson, E., Keane, K., & Khanna, S. (2020). Beyond decoding: A meta-analysis of the effects of language comprehension interventions on K–5 students' language and literacy outcomes. *Reading Research Quarterly, 55*, S207–S233.

Spear-Swerling, L. (2016). Common types of reading problems and how to help children who have them. *The Reading Teacher, 69*(5), 513–522.

Stanovich, K. E. (1980). Toward an interactive-compensatory model of individual differences in the development of reading fluency. *Reading Research Quarterly*, 32–71.

Stanovich, K. E. (2009). Matthew effects in reading: Some consequences of individual differences in the acquisition of literacy. *Journal of Education, 189*(1-2), 23–55.

Stockard, J., Wood, T. W., Coughlin, C., & Rasplica Khoury, C. (2018). The effectiveness of direct instruction curricula: A meta-analysis of a half century of research. *Review of Educational Research, 88*(4), 479–507.

Suggate, S. P. (2016). A meta-analysis of the long-term effects of phonemic awareness, phonics, fluency, and reading comprehension interventions. *Journal of Learning Disabilities, 49*(1), 77–96.

Sunde, K., Furnes, B., & Lundetræ, K. (2020). Does introducing the letters faster boost the development of children's letter knowledge, word reading and spelling in the first year of school?. *Scientific Studies of Reading, 24*(2), 141–158.

Taylor, B. M., Pearson, P. D., Clark, K., & Walpole, S. (2000). Effective schools and accomplished teachers: Lessons about primary-grade reading instruction in low-income schools. *The Elementary School Journal, 101*(2), 121–165.

Therrien, W. J., Wickstrom, K., & Jones, K. (2006). Effect of a combined repeated reading and question generation intervention on reading achievement. *Learning Disabilities Research & Practice, 21*(2), 89–97.

Torgerson, C., Brooks, G., Gascoine, L., & Higgins, S. (2018). Phonics: reading policy and the evidence of effectiveness from a systematic 'tertiary' review. *Research Papers in Education, 34*(2), 208–238.

Torppa, M., Georgiou, G. K., Lerkkanen, M. K., Niemi, P., Poikkeus, A. M., & Nurmi, J. E. (2016). Examining the simple view of reading in a transparent orthography: A longitudinal study from kindergarten to grade 3. *Merrill-Palmer Quarterly (1982-), 62*(2), 179–206.

Tortorelli, L. S. (2019). Reading rate in informational text: Norms and implications for theory and practice in the primary grades. *Reading Psychology, 40*(3), 293–324.

Toste, J. R., Williams, K. J., & Capin, P. (2017). Reading big words: Instructional practices to promote multisyllabic word reading fluency. *Intervention in School and Clinic, 52*(5), 270–278.

Toste, J. R., Didion, L., Peng, P., Filderman, M. J., & McClelland, A. M. (2020). A meta-analytic review of the relations between motivation and reading achievement for K–12 students. *Review of Educational Research, 90*(3), 420–456.

Treiman, R., Tincoff, R., Rodriguez, K., Mouzaki, A., & Francis, D. J. (1998). The foundations of literacy: Learning the sounds of letters. *Child Development, 69*(6), 1524–1540.

Treiman, R., Hulslander, J., Olson, R. K., Willcutt, E. G., Byrne, B., & Kessler, B. (2019). The unique role of early spelling in the prediction of later literacy performance. *Scientific Studies of Reading, 23*(5), 437–444.

Tuan, L. T. (2010). Teaching English discrete sounds through minimal pairs. *Journal of Language Teaching and Research, 1*(5), 540.

Ukrainetz, T. A., Cooney, M. H., Dyer, S. K., Kysar, A. J., & Harris, T. J. (2000). An investigation into teaching phonemic awareness through shared reading and writing. *Early Childhood Research Quarterly, 15*(3), 331–355.

Vadasy, P. F., & Sanders, E. A. (2021). Introducing grapheme-phoneme correspondences (GPCs): exploring rate and complexity in phonics instruction for kindergarteners with limited literacy skills. *Reading and Writing, 34*(1), 109–138.

Vadasy, P. F., Sanders, E. A., & Peyton, J. A. (2006). Code-oriented instruction for kindergarten students at risk for reading difficulties: A randomized field trial with paraeducator implementers. *Journal of Educational Psychology, 98*(3), 508.

Wesseling, P. B., Christmann, C. A., & Lachmann, T. (2017). Shared book reading promotes not only language development, but also grapheme awareness in German kindergarten children. *Frontiers in Psychology, 8*, 1–14.

White, T. G., Sabatini, J. P., & White, S. (2021). What does "below basic" mean on NAEP reading?. *Educational Researcher, 50*(8), 570–573.

Williams, R., & Morris, R. (2004). Eye movements, word familiarity, and vocabulary acquisition. *European Journal of Cognitive Psychology, 16*(1-2), 312–339.

Wolters, A. P., Kim, Y. S. G., & Szura, J. W. (2020). Is reading prosody related to reading comprehension? A meta-analysis. *Scientific Studies of Reading*, 1–20.

Yap, M. J., & Balota, D. A. (2009). Visual word recognition of multisyllabic words. *Journal of Memory and Language, 60*, 502–529.

Zemlock, D., Vinci-Booher, S., & James, K. H. (2018). Visual–motor symbol production facilitates letter recognition in young children. *Reading and Writing, 31*(6), 1255–1271.

Zhang, D., & Ke, S. (2020). The simple view of reading made complex by morphological decoding fluency in bilingual fourth-grade readers of English. *Reading Research Quarterly, 55*(2), 311–329. https://doi.org/10.1002/rrq.287

Zucker, T. A., Cabell, S. Q., Justice, L. M., Pentimonti, J. M., & Kaderavek, J. N. (2013). The role of frequent, interactive prekindergarten shared reading in the longitudinal development of language and literacy skills. *Developmental Psychology, 49*(8), 1425–1439.

INDEX

READING ABOVE THE FRAY